HAITI

Roseline Ng Cheong-Lum

MARSHALL CAVENDISH
New York • London • Sydney

Reference edition published 1995 by
Marshall Cavendish Corporation
2415 Jerusalem Avenue
P.O. Box 587
North Bellmore
New York 11710

© Times Editions Pte Ltd 1995

Originated and designed by
Times Books International, an imprint of
Times Editions Pte Ltd

Printed in Singapore

Library of Congress Cataloging-in-Publication Data:
Cheong-Lum, Roseline Ng.
  Haiti / Roseline Ng Cheong-Lum.
    p. cm.—(Cultures Of The World)
  Includes bibliographical references and index.
  ISBN 1-85435-693-3 :
    1. Haiti—Juvenile literature [1. Haiti.] I. Title.
II. Series.
F1915.2.C44 1994
972.94—dc20   94–22572
                        CIP
                         AC

Cultures of the World
Editorial Director	Shirley Hew
Managing Editor	Shova Loh
Editors	Elizabeth Berg
	Jacquiline King
	Dinah Lee
	Azra Moiz
	Sue Sismondo
Picture Editor	Susan Jane Manuel
Production	Anthony Chua
Design	Tuck Loong
	Ronn Yeo
	Felicia Wong
	Loo Chuan Ming
Illustrators	Anuar
	Chow Kok Keong
	William Sim
MCC Editorial Director	Evelyn M. Fazio
MCC Production Manager	Janet Castiglioni

INTRODUCTION

HAITI HAS BEEN described as *un pays tête-en-bas* ("uhn pay-EE teht-ahn-BAH"), a country turned upside down. The first black republic in the Western world, Haiti's past is bathed in the blood spilled in a fight for freedom, democracy, and a better standard of living. Once the richest colony in the Americas, Haiti is now the poorest country in the Western Hemisphere. Yet Haitians have retained an optimism and a *joie de vivre* ("djwad VEE-vre") characteristic of the Caribbean. Their voodoo religion is a celebration of their African roots and is expressed through dance and song. Their surroundings, from humble thatched huts to ornate colonial mansions, are a riot of color. Living in close-knit communities, Haitians work hard and help each other. This volume of *Cultures of the World* explores the different aspects of the Haitian way of life, and demonstrates the fortitude and perseverance of a people faced with adversity.

CONTENTS

Grouper, mullet, tuna, anchovies, and sea bass abound in Haiti's coastal waters.

CONTENTS

Haitians are known for their cheerful and friendly nature.

GEOGRAPHY

THE REPUBLIC OF HAITI consists of the western third of the island of Hispaniola, the second largest island in the Caribbean. The other two-thirds belong to the Dominican Republic.

The island of Hispaniola, together with Cuba, Puerto Rico and Jamaica, form the Greater Antilles, one of the four island chains that make up the West Indies.

Lying 565 miles southeast of Florida, Hispaniola is separated from Puerto Rico on the east by the Mona Passage and from Cuba on the west by the Windward Passage. These two passages are the principal water routes linking North America and Europe with South and Central America.

Covering a total area of 10,710 square miles—only slightly larger than the state of Maryland—Haiti has a northern and a southern peninsula separated by the Gulf of Gonâve. The shape of Haiti has been compared to a lobster's claw, with the upper pincer pointing toward Cuba, and the lower, longer claw toward Jamaica.

Above: **A palm tree lined beach is a common sight in Haiti and throughout the Caribbean.**

Opposite: **Haitian children enjoy the panoramic view from one of the country's many mountainsides.**

The Haitian landscape is characterized by broad bands of towering mountain ranges, interspersed with fertile lowland plains and lakes. The island's geographical position ensures that natural disasters such as earthquakes, landslides, and tropical storms are a fairly frequent occurrence. Natural resources, on the other hand, are limited—most of the country has been denuded of its forests, the bauxite mining industry has collapsed, and the search for oil has been unsuccessful.

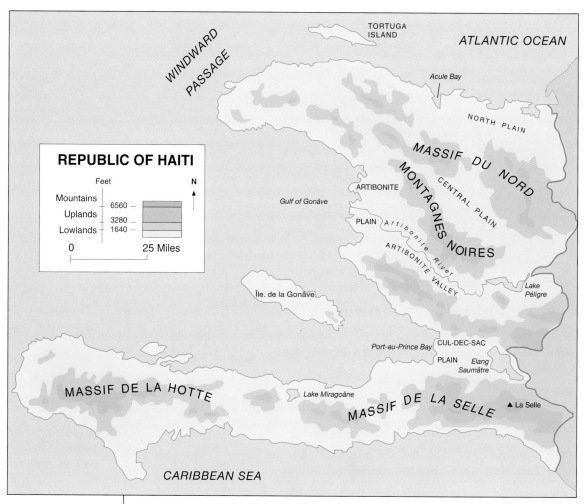

MOUNTAIN RANGES AND PLAINS

The word "Haiti," in the language of the Arawaks, the first inhabitants of the island, means "mountainous land." The country is dominated by three mountain ranges; when added together, Haiti's highland regions cover more than three-quarters of the land area. Less than 20% of the land lies below 600 feet, while 40% rises above 1,500 feet.

The longest mountain range, the Massif du Nord, runs southeastward from the Atlantic coast and crosses the border with the Dominican Republic, where it changes its name to the Cordillera Central. Haiti's highest peak is La Selle, which at 8,793 feet dominates the Massif de la Selle mountain range.

Mountain Ranges and Plains

The Central Plain extends over 840 square miles from the Montagnes Noires, south of the Massif du Nord, to the border with the Dominican Republic, while the North Plain covers 150 square miles between the Massif du Nord and the Atlantic Ocean. This area, with its rich and fertile soil, was the plantation heartland during the French colonial period. Two smaller plains, the Artibonite and the Cul-de-Sac, border the Gulf of Gonâve.

Every inch of arable land is cultivated and even very steep mountain slopes are tilled. Numerous stories are told of farmers falling to their deaths from their cornfields. Much of Haiti suffers from extensive erosion due to over-cultivation, and a muddy brown ring surrounds the country's coastline where the topsoil has washed into the sea.

"The high and rocky mountains on either side of the harbor rose from among noble forests and swept down into luxuriant plains and cultivated fields ..."

—Christopher Columbus as he sighted the northern tip of Haiti

More than three-quarters of Haiti's people live in the agricultural plains and valleys.

THE MOVING BORDER

Haiti's 193-mile border with the Dominican Republic follows mountain ridges and streams from the north to the south of the island. Along a stretch of the interior highlands, the frontier is defined by the International Route, a highway running parallel to the Libon River. Before the construction of the road, the river itself served as the border.

The valleys provide easy access between the island's two countries, with the result that the migration of Haitians to the Dominican Republic has always been high—Haitian farmers suffering from a lack of land at home have always looked longingly at the vast, empty stretches of land beyond the border. By settling on parts of that land and claiming them for Haiti, they pushed the border farther into the Dominican Republic.

When the practice became widespread, the Haitian government stepped in and tried to reinstate the original border, but the presence of military guards has not succeeded in halting the flow of Haitians into the Dominican Republic.

TROPICAL FLORA

A few hundred years ago, Haiti was covered with marshes of wild ginger, plantations of bananas and Indian corn, and tropical rainforests of mahogany, redwood, and pine. Now the landscape looks quite different: the plantations were subdivided after independence, while the vast expanses of trees gradually disappeared as more and more land was cleared to provide agricultural land for an ever-increasing population. Haiti is one of the few countries in the world where the destruction of the original woodland is almost complete. Surviving pine and hardwood trees now grow only on the upper levels of the mountains.

Haiti boasts a wide variety of flowering tropical trees and shrubs.

Mangroves fringe the Gulf of Gonâve and the Atlantic coast to the east of Cap-Haïtien. Elsewhere along the coastline, thickets of guava fruit grow in profusion. The North Plain supports scattered patches of desert-like growth; here, trees grow only along the edges of rivers and streams. In the northwestern reaches of the Central Plain, the grasslands are dotted with semideciduous trees and conifers; the southeastern part is covered with scrub woodland and cacti. In the Artibonite Plain, thorny scrub woodland near the coast gives way to grassland savanna and mixed woodland farther inland.

Tropical flowers, such as wild orchids, royal poincianas, bougainvillea, poinsettias, and frangipani, provide stunning color, beauty, and fragrance. Native fruit trees include avocado, orange, lime, and cherry. About 20 species of plants that grow indigenously are useful for their nutritional or medicinal properties.

18th century travelers were stunned by Haiti's lush tropical foliage, but 200 years of deforestation has destroyed much of the greenery.

11

The slender and beautiful Greater Flamingo breeds in Haiti's marshy lowland lakes.

FAUNA

Indigenous to Haiti are several types of reptiles, including three varieties of crocodile, the rhino-horned iguana, small lizards, and nonpoisonous snakes. Insects abound, as well as spiders, scorpions, and centipedes. These are all poisonous, but their stings are rarely fatal.

As recently as the 1960s, Haiti was a bird-lover's paradise: spotted sandpipers, roseate flamingos, long-billed curlews, peregrine falcons, and black-bellied plovers all flourished. Deforestation has destroyed the habitat of many of these species, but parrots, wild pigeons, guinea hens, ducks, and weaver birds can still be found. Egrets and flamingos make their nests around the brackish lakes of the Cul-de-Sac Plain.

The waters along the coast of Haiti and the numerous rivers support various species of fish. There are 270 species of fish in the coastal waters, including tarpon, kingfish, barracuda, and red snapper.

NATURE'S FURY

Hurricanes occur when a drop in atmospheric pressure is accompanied by unstable air currents. In the Caribbean, winds spiral in a clockwise direction toward the storm center. The "eye" of the hurricane is an area of low pressure, which is very calm.

In the Caribbean, hurricanes form in the waters east of the Lesser Antilles and travel in a general northwesterly direction, hugging the North American coast. The most destructive hurricane this century was Flora, which knocked several islands on its path, killing over 7,000 people and causing damage worth $500 million in the region.

CLIMATE

Haiti's climate is hot and dry all year round. Temperatures vary slightly with elevation: the annual average is 81°F in the lowlands and 76°F in the highland interior. On the coast, sea breezes temper the tropical heat. The hottest months are June through September, while the coolest are from February to April.

The mountains surrounding valleys form protective walls that, when coupled with direct sunlight, can produce the country's highest temperatures. Haiti's capital, Port-au-Prince, is sheltered by mountains to the north and south. It is one of the hottest cities in the Caribbean.

Haiti lies in a rain shadow and generally receives less rainfall than its neighbor, the Dominican Republic. Rainfall produced by trade winds is stopped by the mountain ridge dividing the two countries. The north of Haiti receives the most rain—between 20 and 100 inches per year—but the high rate of evaporation prevents most of the water from seeping into the soil.

June through October is hurricane season in Haiti. Hurricane Flora, nicknamed the "Big Blow," killed 3,000 people in 1963. In 1980, Hurricane Allen caused considerable damage in Haiti's southern peninsula.

Cactus plants offer a perfect alternative to clotheslines in Haiti's hot, dry climate.

RIVERS AND LAKES

More than 100 rivers and streams flow from the mountains into the sea. Although most Haitian rivers are shallow and unnavigable, due to the high rate of evaporation, they are very important for irrigation and for the production of hydroelectricity.

The longest river is the Artibonite River, which is about 10 times longer than the others. Originating in the Cordillera Central in the Dominican Republic, the Artibonite flows 174 miles west across Haiti before emptying into the Gulf of Gonâve. The damming of the upper Artibonite has produced Lake Péligre, a reservoir used for flood control, irrigation, and hydroelectricity.

The largest natural lake in Haiti is the 65 square mile Etang Saumâtre. It is the habitat of many exotic species of tropical wildlife.

The Artibonite is the only river in Haiti that is even partially navigable.

More than a million Haitians live in the bustling capital city of Port-au-Prince.

CITIES AND TOWNS

PORT-AU-PRINCE Founded in 1749 and rebuilt several times after earthquakes and fires, Haiti's capital city today bears little resemblance to the original French colonial town, although its architecture still retains a distinctive French flavor. The streets of Port-au-Prince reveal the extreme contrasts between rich and poor that are characteristic of Haiti: dirty, dusty, and overcrowded shantytowns stand side by side with elegant mansions and gleaming public buildings.

JACMEL French colonialist Jacques de Melo founded this provincial town on Haiti's south coast in 1689. Once a flourishing town that traded with Europe in coffee, orange peel (for the French liqueur Cointreau), and cotton, Jacmel is now in decline. It has only 217,000 inhabitants, even though it is Haiti's second largest city.

HISTORY

HAITI HAS THE DISTINCTION of being the first black independent republic in the Americas, winning its freedom from France less than 30 years after the United States gained its independence. Despite this early liberation and a national motto that boldly proclaims "Strength Through Union," Haiti has continued to endure a tumultuous history characterized by enormous struggle and bloodshed. After almost 200 years of rule by a series of despotic emperors, eccentric kings, cruel dictators, powerless presidents, and tyrannical generals, nothing has really improved for the average Haitian. In early 1994, Haiti was a country with severe economic and social problems, and no real prospect of change.

Haitians today are still fighting for the freedom and civil liberties they were hoping for when they overthrew the colonial authorities.

Opposite: **A young man celebrates the demise of Haitian dictator "Baby Doc" in 1986.**

Left: **The enormous Citadelle Laferrière was built by King Henri Christophe.**

PRE-COLUMBIAN TIMES

The island of Hispaniola was inhabited from around 5000 B.C. by Paleo-Indians, a group of hunter-gatherers who are believed to have come from

Central America. In 1000 B.C., Meso-Indians spread from South America into the islands of the Greater Antilles. Hunter-gatherers too, they also knew how to make tools and pottery. By the time Christopher Columbus arrived in the 15th century, Hispaniola was inhabited by the Arawaks, a gentle and peace-loving tribe of Indians who called themselves Taíno, "the Good People."

HISPANIOLA

Haiti's earliest inhabitants were two Indian tribes, the Arawaks and the Caribs.

Christopher Columbus "discovered" Hispaniola on his first voyage to the Americas in 1492. It was one of the first islands he encountered, and he named it *La Isla Española* ("lah EES-lah ess-pah-NYOH-lah," or The Spanish Island, later anglicized to Hispaniola) and claimed it for the kingdom of Spain. The Arawaks he met were friendly and offered gold ornaments to him and his crew. When Columbus returned to Europe, he left 40 men on Hispaniola with orders to look for gold.

While Columbus prepared for his second expedition to the New World, a warlike tribe of Indians called the Caribs (the Arawak word for "cannibal") moved north through the Caribbean from South America. They massacred the Arawaks they found on Hispaniola and destroyed the

Spanish fort there. When Columbus returned, he established a new settlement on the south coast of Hispaniola, in what is now the Dominican Republic. Thus was established the first permanent European colony in the Americas. The Spaniards called it Santo Domingo.

Subsequently, more settlers arrived from Spain and were granted large tracts of land to use as they pleased. They established sugar plantations and made the Indians their slaves. Hard labor and European diseases took their toll on the indigenous population and by the mid-16th century the number of Indians had declined from one million to 5,000. The labor shortage for the plantations grew acute and the colonialists began to ship large numbers of slaves to Haiti from Africa. By 1520, almost all laborers on Hispaniola were African slaves.

In 1535, Hispaniola became part of the Viceroyalty of New Spain, which included Central America and much of North America. The Spanish conquistadores used Hispaniola as a base for exploring the region. When news of the discovery of large quantities of gold in Mexico and Peru reached the settlers, they abandoned Santo Domingo. Spain soon lost interest in Hispaniola.

When he first saw Hispaniola, Columbus thought he had found China or India.

19

Old French mortars stand as a reminder of Haiti's colonial past.

In the 18th century, Saint Domingue was the richest colony in the French Empire and was known as the Pearl of the Antilles.

THE FRENCH COLONY OF SAINT DOMINGUE

Around 1625, English and French pirates established a base on Tortuga Island off the north coast of Haiti to launch their attacks on the gold-laden Spanish galleons sailing from Central America to Europe.

Sixteen years later, the buccaneers moved to the mainland and founded the settlement of Port Margot on the north-west tip of the island. Soon after, the French drove out the English and renamed the settlement Saint Domingue.

The French concentrated on two extremely profitable activities—farming and piracy—and Saint Domingue quickly prospered. In 1697, the Spanish ceded the western third of Hispaniola to France under the Treaty of Ryswick, while retaining control of the eastern two-thirds.

The French colonialists successfully grew sugarcane, coffee, cocoa, cotton, and indigo on vast plantations worked by half a million African slaves. A fleet of 700 ships carrying annual exports worth $40 million sailed between Saint Domingue and Europe. Saint Domingue was soon the most profitable slave colony in the world, contributing much of the wealth of major French ports such as Marseille.

Saint Domingue's plantation owners, known as *grands blancs* ("grahn BLAHN"), literally "great white men," also acquired enormous wealth and lived a luxurious life that was the envy of all of Europe. The capital of the colony, Cap Français, was regarded as the Paris of the New World.

By this time, several thousand mulatto *affranchis* ("ah-frahn-SHEE"), or "freemen," had also become the owners of large sugar plantations. *Affranchis* were Haitians of mixed African and European descent who had won their freedom from slavery and had been granted French citizenship. Despite their considerable wealth, these "freemen" were still not treated as equals by the white planters, and hostilities between the two groups increased.

PIRATES AND BUCCANEERS

In the first half of the 17th century, a group of French and English pirates and buccaneers took refuge on Tortuga Island after being driven off the Caribbean island of St. Christopher by the Spanish. The small community was soon joined by Dutch refugees. The early buccaneers were escaped servants, former soldiers, and logwood cutters from what is now southern Mexico. Together, they hunted wild boar and cattle, and cultivated crops.

Buccaneers acquired their name from their custom of curing meat on spits called *boucans* ("boo-CAHN"). But each nationality also had their own term for the adventurers—the French called them *flibustiers* ("flih-buhss-TEEAY," from the Dutch word for freebooter), the Dutch *zeerovers* ("see-ROH-vehrs," or sea rovers), and the Spanish *corsarios* ("kohr-SAH-riohs"). Their stories influenced such authors as Jonathan Swift, Daniel Defoe, and Robert Louis Stevenson.

To combat attacks by the Spaniards, the buccaneers banded together and called themselves the Brethren of the Coast. The more aggressive ones engaged in piracy against Spanish ships. Tortuga Island, 10 miles out to sea from Port-de-Paix on the northeastern coast of Haiti, was an ideal launching pad for attacks on Spanish ships transporting gold between Central America and Europe. Working in small crews, the pirates became known for their extreme cruelty. England, France, and the Netherlands did nothing to prevent the pirate attacks, as they were eager to break Spain's trade monopoly. Buccaneering finally came to an end in 1689.

SLAVE REVOLT

"Hidden God in a cloud
is there, watching us.
He sees all the whites do;
the Whitegod demands crimes
ours wants good things.
But our God that is so good
orders vengeance, he will
ride us, assist us.
Throw away the thoughts of
the Whitegod who thirsts
for our tears, listen to
freedom that speaks from our hearts."

With this invocation at a voodoo ceremony at Bois-Caiman on August 14, 1791, Bookman Dutty, a voodoo priest, urged his countrymen to rise up in arms. One week later, 50,000 insurgents seized control of the important North Plain for 10 days, killing 1,000 whites and destroying the country's sugar plantations. Uprisings broke out throughout the country, with women fighting alongside the men. At least 10,000 slaves died.

FIRST BLACK REPUBLIC IN THE WEST

In 1789, the French Revolution's proclamation of "equality among all men," led the *affranchis* to push for their own equality with the white planters in Saint Domingue. A mulatto demonstration in 1791 resulted in riots and a major slave rebellion. The rebellion was led by Toussaint L'Ouverture, a former slave, grandson of an African chieftain, and a first-class military strategist with considerable leadership qualities who quickly moved up the ranks of the French army. As a result of the rebellion, slavery was abolished in Saint Domingue in 1793.

Spanish and British invaders attempted to take control of the sugar plantations that were destroyed during the slave revolt, but Toussaint *(handwritten note)* Toussaint L'Ouverture pgs 22-24

L'Ouverture and his *army successfully repelled the invading forces.* Meanwhile, Santo Dom*ingo, the eastern two-thirds of Hispaniola, failed* to flourish under Spanis*h rule, and in 1795, Spain ceded their share of the* island to France under *the Treaty of Basle.*

In 1801, Toussaint L'Ouverture appointed himself governor-for-life of both Saint Domingue and Santo Domingo, but it was independence from France and the abolition of slavery throughout the island that he truly desired. Toussaint freed the slaves in Santo Domingo but stopped short of declaring the independence of Hispaniola.

Napoleon, intent on expanding his empire even further, was not prepared to lose such a valuable slave colony. He sent a huge army and fleet of ships to Hispaniola to overthrow Toussaint L'Ouverture and restore slavery in Santo Domingo. Napoleon's army did succeed in capturing Toussaint and shipping him off to France as a prisoner, but underestimated the strength and fervor of Haitian nationalist forces led by army generals Henri Christophe, Jean-Jacques Dessalines, and Alexandre Pétion. Yellow fever contributed to the downfall of the French, and they surrendered to Dessalines in 1803.

On January 1, 1804, Dessalines proclaimed the independence of Saint Domingue. The first black republic in the New World was renamed Haiti.

Haitian forces battle French soldiers in the 1803 struggle for independence.

THE OPENER

Born in 1743, Toussaint was a slave luckier than many others because his master allowed him to learn to read and write, and even to borrow his books. As a child, he had to work in the fields together with the other slaves. But his reading and conversations with the other slaves gave him the knowledge of other lands where people were free and happy. A man of superior intellect, Toussaint learned the secrets of medicinal herbs and plants, and how to treat sick people with them. He was soon well known among the slaves.

When Toussaint was in his 40s, the slave rebellion broke out and he decided to join the insurgents. As one of the few slaves who could read and write, he was a natural choice for the

leadership. Toussaint had never been to military school, but his reading had given him a great knowledge of military tactics; he always made careful plans, taking his enemies by surprise and outmaneuvering them.

In 1793, France agreed to free the slaves in Saint Domingue, although Saint Domingue was to remain a French colony. Toussaint then became a general in the French army, fighting against the British and the Spanish who were attacking Saint Domingue by land and by sea. In 1801, he declared himself governor-for-life. Napoleon, who came to power in France in 1799, refused to recognize Toussaint's abolition of slavery in Santo Domingo and sent a large army to fight the newly emancipated slaves.

After a few months of resistance, Toussaint was tricked into boarding a French boat where he was arrested. He was taken to France and thrown into a medieval castle prison high in the mountains near the Swiss border. He died there of pneumonia two years later. Upon his deportation from Haiti, Toussaint vowed that the struggle for freedom would continue: "In overthrowing me, they have cut down in Saint Domingue the trunk of the tree of black liberty. It will shoot up again through the roots, for they are numerous and deep."

Toussaint got his nickname *L'Ouverture* ("loo-vair-TOOR," the opening) in the days of the rebellion. Some say that it was because he opened up the way to freedom for the black people, while other people say it was because he was so good at opening moves in battle. Still others believe that it referred to the wide gap between his two front teeth.

EMPERORS AND KINGS

After independence, General Jean-Jacques Dessalines proclaimed himself Jean-Jacques the First, Emperor of Haiti. A cruel leader, he ordered the killing of most of the whites still on Haiti. He was assassinated in 1806, and it was then that civil war broke out between mulattoes, led by Alexandre Pétion, and blacks, led by Henri Christophe. Christophe took control of the north, crowned himself King of Haiti, and set about building palaces and fortresses. He suffered a stroke in 1820 and committed suicide soon after. Alexandre Pétion was president of the south until his death in 1818. The country was then united again under President Jean-Pierre Boyer who governed until 1843. Unrest and turmoil soon began again, however, and Haiti saw 22 heads of state in the next 72 years. Most of these leaders were forced out of office by violent means.

Faustin Soulouque became ruler of Haiti when his name was drawn out of a hat. He declared himself Emperor Faustin I.

King Henri Christophe built the Sans Souci Palace as a private retreat. His court included such titles as the Count of Lemonade and the Count of Marmalade.

THE AMERICAN OCCUPATION

In 1915, after Haitian presidents had been murdered or deposed in four consecutive years, the United States sent Marines to Haiti to protect its business interests there from local upheaval and to protect its strategic interests in the region—World War I had started the year before. The Haitian government signed a treaty with the United States, agreeing to U.S. economic and political assistance. Originally intended to last 10 years, this treaty was extended another 10 years.

Although the United States built an extensive infrastructure, set up medical facilities, and made large loans to the Haitian government, the Haitian people soon grew resentful of the occupiers. Haitians were treated as inferiors—they were barred from public office and were used as enforced labor on road-building projects—and there were several attempts at rebellion.

American troops finally withdrew from Haiti in 1934, but the United States continued to exert direct fiscal control until 1941. Indirect control was lifted in 1947.

THE DUVALIER YEARS

Resentment against the American occupation has not prevented Haitians from using U.S. goods to make a living.

When the Americans left, Haiti was again in turmoil, with frequent coups, revolutions, dictatorships, and street violence, until the election of François Duvalier in 1957. Duvalier, a conservative black doctor and student of voodoo, promised to restore power to the blacks. He was hailed as a liberator and affectionately called "Papa Doc."

Papa Doc's rule soon turned into one of repression and fear. With the help of his personal and brutal police force, the *Tontons macoute* ("tohn-tohn mah-COOT"), he created an environment that kept the Haitian people in a constant state of terror. A fanatical dictator, Papa Doc became known as "Lucifer of the Antilles." Haiti was shunned by the rest of the world, and many of the country's educated and wealthy mulattoes emigrated.

Although originally elected for a term of six years, Papa Doc declared himself president-for-life in 1964. In 1971, just before he died, he changed the constitution to enable him to designate his 19-year-old son Jean-Claude, or "Baby Doc," as his successor.

Baby Doc slackened the repression just enough to gain international respectability and the restoration of U.S. aid. Despite this and a short-term revival of the tourist industry during the 1970s, Haiti's economy stagnated. While Baby Doc and his aristocratic mulatto

Papa Doc always dressed in black. The Duvalier family and associates are alleged to have embezzled $120 million from Haiti.

wife Michèle Bennett lived an extravagant lifestyle in the National Palace, most of the Haitian people slipped deeper and deeper into poverty. Thousands of Haitians from all walks of life fled the country in search of greener pastures.

Hostility toward the excesses of the Duvalier regime and the worsening poverty increased during the early 1980s. In 1985, 60,000 youths demonstrated with the rallying cry, "We would rather die on our feet than live on our knees." Despite a full show of force by the *Tontons macoute*, Jean-Claude Duvalier and his family had no choice but to flee the country in 1986.

BLOOD BATH IN JÉRÉMIE

August 11, 1964: Pierre Sansaricq, along with seven others, is arrested by the *Tontons macoute.* A few days later, the prisoners are released, except for Pierre. He does not know why he is arrested. He has always been charitable in his community and has even given food to the *macoutes* on those days they were not paid by Duvalier. He is executed, but first he is dragged to his office and forced to open his safe for the *macoutes* to help themselves.

September 19, 1964: At 8 p.m., the *macoutes* are in Jérémie again. This time they have come to arrest the whole Sansaricq family, including four young children. The prisoners are immediately taken to the execution ground without even the pretense of a trial. When they are offered blindfolds, the whole family refuses to wear them. The graves have already been dug a few yards away.

One of the executioners, feeling a sudden stab of pity for the children, asks the leader to give him the youngest child. In response the leader plants his knife right into the heart of the toddler. The mother rushes forward and is shot repeatedly. The four-year-old brother asks to go to the bathroom. Sony Borges, one of the *macoutes*, takes him by the hand and thrusts his lighted cigarette into the eyes of the young boy. At the same time another one stabs him with the same knife that killed his sister. The other prisoners are disposed of quickly.

FAILED ATTEMPTS AT DEMOCRACY

After the ousting of Jean-Claude Duvalier, a National Council of Government was established under the army chief Lieutenant General Henri Namphy. Although the council dissolved the pro-Duvalier legislature and—officially, at least—disbanded the *Tontons macoute*, it could not cope with the ensuing political and economic chaos. A new constitution was approved in March 1987, providing for a president, a prime minister, and a two-chamber legislature. The first elections in nearly three decades were held in 1988, but there were allegations of widespread fraud and less than 10% of Haitians turned out to vote.

After several coups d'état, the Haitian population again went to the polls in January 1991. To the great jubilation of the Haitian people, Jean-Bertrand Aristide, a Roman Catholic priest, was elected with 67% of the vote. He lost no time in implementing land reform, combating illiteracy, controlling the army, and shrinking the bureaucracy, but these actions alienated the upper class and the army. In an army-led revolt in September 1991, Aristide was abducted and deported to Venezuela. The international

THE BOAT PEOPLE

So desperate were the Haitian people for freedom in the 1980s and early 1990s that tens of thousands crowded onto unseaworthy wooden boats bound for the United States. Some were caught and detained by the Haitian authorities before they could even set sail, while many others lost their lives at sea. Most of those who did manage to reach American shores were seized by the U.S. Coast Guard and returned to Haiti under the terms of a refugee-return agreement. In November 1991, a U.S. federal court judge ordered the repatriation to cease, but this was repealed by the Bush administration and more than 6,000 Haitians were moved to the U.S. naval base at Guantánamo Bay in Cuba. Despite an appeal by the United Nations Commission on Human Rights, they were repatriated to Haiti in February 1992. The Clinton administration has continued the repatriation policy, with one significant change: it now accepts political refugees—the targets of political persecution in Haiti. It is not known how permanent this policy will be.

community quickly responded by cutting off aid and imposing a trade embargo. It has tried to negotiate the return of Aristide, who is currently in the United States, but the intransigence of the Haitian military has so far resulted in deadlock.

GOVERNMENT

WHEN HAITI BROKE FREE of French rule in 1804, there were high hopes for this predominantly black republic. But after nearly two centuries of independence, the Haitian people are still struggling to achieve true democracy. The country's constitution, originally based on the French Napoleonic Code and the U.S. Constitution, has been changed many times over the years, mainly to reinforce the positions of those in power. Virtual dictatorship has been the rule for the last 40 years, since François Duvalier—better known as "Papa Doc"—declared himself president-for-life and then passed the title down to his son, "Baby Doc." After the collapse of the Duvalier regime, Haitian politics were marked by a series of coup d'états, rigged elections, and martial law. Since President Jean-Bertrand Aristide was ousted in 1991, Haiti has effectively been under military rule.

For many decades, corrupt government officials have drained public funds, helping to keep the Haitian people in poverty.

Opposite: **A supporter of Jean-Bertrand Aristide, now Haitian president-in-exile in the United States, wears a pro-Aristide "rooster hat."**

Left: **A young boy stands before a mural of Aristide.**

31

The National Palace is one of several stately public buildings that surround the Place des Héros de l'Indépendence, a palm-fringed plaza that is the heart of Haitian civic and national life.

NATIONAL GOVERNMENT

The Haitian constitution adopted in March 1987 declares Haiti to be a republic with three branches of government: executive, legislative, and judicial.

THE EXECUTIVE Executive power is shared by the president of the republic, who is directly elected for a term of five years, and the prime minister, who is chosen by the president with the approval of the National Assembly. The president is barred from serving more than two consecutive terms.

THE LEGISLATURE The Haitian Parliament, like the U.S. Congress, is made up of two houses: the 27-seat Senate and the 83-seat Chamber of Deputies. Members of both houses are elected by a national vote for a term of five years.

THE JUDICIARY Haitian law is based on the French Napoleonic Code, with certain modifications made by the Duvalier regime. The judicial system has four levels: the Court of Cassation, the Court of Appeal, civil courts, and magistrates' courts. The Court of Cassation is similar to the U.S. Supreme Court, and judges for both the Court of Cassation and the

Court of Appeal are appointed by the president for a period of 10 years. They may not be removed from office unless found guilty of misconduct. Judges for civil and magistrates' courts serve for seven years.

LOCAL GOVERNMENT

Haiti is divided into nine departments that are responsible for the administration of local government. The nine departments are further divided into about 100 communes. Each department has its own capital, and each commune has a *bourg* ("BOOR"), a major town with municipal authority, and five or six *sections rurales* ("sec-SIOHN ruh-RAHL"), or rural districts. The latter are administered by local district leaders appointed by the government.

Lieutenant General Henri Namphy ruled Haiti after the overthrow of Baby Doc in 1986.

POLITICAL FORCES

The largest and most powerful group within the National Assembly is the pro-Aristide *Front National pour le Changement et la Démocratie* ("frohn nah-sioh-NAHL poor luh shahnge-MAHN," or FNCD). The FNCD was formed when a group of leftwing parties and popular organizations joined forces for the 1990 presidential and legislative elections. In 1991, they increased their strength, winning 38 seats in the Chamber of Deputies and 13 in the Senate.

CONSTITUTIONAL REFORM

The 1987 constitution includes many provisions intended to safeguard the democratic rights of the Haitian people. It provides for:

- the equality of all Haitians before the law,
- full political rights, including the right to vote, for all Haitians over the age of 21,
- freedom of the press and freedom of thought,
- the recognition of Creole as an official language,
- the recognition of voodoo as an official religion,
- the separation of the military and the police,
- an independent electoral commission,
- an independent judiciary,
- the abolition of the death penalty,
- a 10-year ban on former officials of the Duvalier regime holding office.

In reality, however, many of these reforms have failed to materialize, and the constitution has been partially or fully suspended several times since it came into effect.

THE HAITIAN FLAG

During colonial days the Haitian flag was the same as the French flag, consisting of three vertical bands: blue, white, and red. During the Haitian War of Independence, in the city of Arcahaie on May 18, 1803, rebel leader Jean-Jacques Dessalines ripped out the white part of the flag as a symbol of the Haitians' hatred for the white colonizers and replaced the blue band with a black band. In 1818, Jean-Pierre Boyer adopted a new pattern of blue and red horizontal bands and a coat of arms, but François Duvalier changed the bands back to vertical black and red in 1964 when he declared himself president-for-life. At the end of the Duvalier regime in 1986, the pre-Duvalier flag of horizontal bands in blue and red was reintroduced.

THE SEARCH FOR DEMOCRACY

Haitians today are still a long way from enjoying complete democracy. Their first freely elected president, Jean-Bertrand Aristide, is living in exile in the United States, fighting to regain his full presidential powers. From September 1991 to June 1992, the country was led by a figurehead president appointed by the military leaders. Negotiations between the international community and the Haitian army and parliament began soon after, and in July 1993—a few days after a worldwide oil embargo was imposed on Haiti—a deal was worked out that would have seen the return of Aristide by October 30, 1993.

A few weeks before the deadline, the agreement collapsed when Haiti's military leaders blocked Aristide's return and prevented U.S. and Canadian police monitors from landing in Haiti. Meanwhile, Haitian military and police forces stepped up their murder of pro-Aristide politicians and voters. As of April 1994, negotiations were at a standstill, despite the severe effect of the oil embargo on the Haitian economy.

Haitians protest against unemployment, poor living conditions, and a lack of political freedom.

Once again, the army is the main political force in Haiti.

35

ECONOMY

ONCE THE RICHEST slave colony in the world, Haiti is now the poorest country in the Western Hemisphere. Haiti's annual gross domestic product is only $360 per capita. About 90% of the population earns less than $150 a year. The top one percent of the population owns 60% of the most fertile land and receives 44% of the national income. Haiti is a predominantly agricultural country, but the failure of food production to keep up with population growth has led to an increased reliance on food imports and the spread of malnutrition and famine. Light industry, started during the American occupation, experienced healthy growth for some time under the Duvalier regime but has stagnated due to the country's political instability. In recent years, human rights abuses and political corruption have led the international community to cut off Haiti's one lifeline—economic aid.

Opposite: **Young Haitians are more likely to work in the fields than go to school. Agriculture is the main source of work for two-thirds of the rural population.**

Left: **This once-grand house now stands derelict and abandoned.**

37

New irrigation schemes have boosted rice production along the fertile banks of the Artibonite River.

Small farm plots, soil erosion, and inadequate irrigation and transportation have hampered the success of Haiti's agricultural sector.

AGRICULTURE

Agriculture is the largest sector of the Haitian economy, accounting for nearly a third of gross domestic product and employing more than two-thirds of the population. Haitian agriculture is typified by small peasant farms. After independence, large estates were dismantled and redistributed in small plots to thousands of peasants. Plots are becoming smaller and smaller as families subdivide their property among their children. Every square inch of arable land is cultivated, and it is becoming increasingly difficult to get good yields as erosion and over-cultivation take their toll on the soil.

The main export crop is coffee, grown on Haiti's numerous mountain slopes, but worldwide overproduction and a drop in prices have led to a severe decrease in coffee's contribution to Haiti's export earnings. Sugar, which used to be the backbone of the Haitian economy, has also declined in importance. Growing sugarcane requires large tracts of flat land and considerable amounts of rainfall, both of which are in short supply in Haiti.

Most of the sugarcane grown on small farms is ground in rural distilleries to produce a type of rum called *clairin* ("clay-REHN").

Most agricultural workers are engaged in the production of food crops for local consumption. The most important are the staples of the Haitian diet—rice, corn, and yams—and other vegetables and fruits, particularly mangoes.

THE GOURDE: STAPLE FOOD AND UNIT OF CURRENCY

The *gourde* ("GOORD"), or calabash, is a very important vegetable to the Haitian peasant. Its flesh is used in many ways in Haitian cooking, and its shell, when dried, makes a very

versatile container, especially for carrying water. The leaves of the calabash tree (a kind of creeper) can also be eaten. After becoming king of the northern part of Haiti in 1807, Henri Christophe decreed that all calabash trees were the property of the state, and so all *gourdes* had to be bought.

The use of the name "gourde" as a unit of currency has continued ever since. One gourde is divided into 100 kobs. During the American occupation, and in the Duvalier years, the gourde was protected from devaluation by a convention signed with the United States. Today, the official rate is five gourdes to one U.S. dollar, but most money is exchanged at the parallel rate, which was approximately 12 gourdes to one U.S. dollar in late 1993.

MANUFACTURING

Manufacturing is the third most important sector of the economy after agriculture and commerce. Despite strong growth in the late 1970s, the manufacturing sector has shrunk in recent years due to Haiti's continued political instability and the international trade and oil embargo. Foreign earnings from exports have dropped since 1986, but manufactured goods are still Haiti's primary export, accounting for almost two-thirds of earnings in 1992.

More than half of the total work force is female; most women work in the Port-au-Prince area, primarily in markets and garment factories.

The main sources of manufacturing jobs are U.S.-owned assembly plants around Port-au-Prince producing electronics, toys, and sporting goods. Haiti is the world's largest producer of baseballs, supplying all balls used by the American and National Leagues in the United States.

Most of these manufacturing plants were set up in the 1970s when Baby Doc was promoting Haiti as the "Taiwan of the Caribbean" and luring companies with the promise of cheap and abundant labor, generous tax concessions, and an almost nonexistent trade union movement. Many plants have now either moved out of Haiti or are operating on a reduced scale.

Foodstuffs, beverages, household goods, and building materials are manufactured for domestic consumption. The top three manufactured goods in 1992 were cigarettes, detergents, and bath soap.

THE LABOR FORCE

Nearly three-quarters of Haitians are still not part of the formal economy and live by subsistence farming. Most of those who do work for wages are employed in the agricultural sector, making a meager 60 cents a day. Commerce employs 15% of the labor force, while 7% work in manufacturing. The rest are distributed among the service industries, mining, and public institutions.

FOREIGN AID

Haiti is highly dependent on economic aid from abroad, primarily from the United States, which supplied over a third of Haiti's foreign aid between 1982 and 1987. Since then, political turmoil in Haiti has disrupted the flow of aid. The United States, Germany, and France all pledged aid packages in mid-1991, only to suspend them following the September 1991 military coup. The resumption of aid was part of the agreement between Haiti and the international community to return President Aristide from exile in October 1993, but it never materialized because the Haitian military failed to keep its side of the bargain. The United States, Canada, and the European Community have yet again pledged substantial amounts in food, reconstruction, and humanitarian aid—conditional upon Aristide's return—but a total impasse in negotiations on this issue makes it unlikely that the Haitian people and economy will see a rapid end to their suffering.

Mining now plays a very small part in the Haitian economy, employing only one percent of the working population.

41

INTERNATIONAL EMBARGOES

When freely-elected President Jean-Bertrand Aristide was ousted from power in 1991, the Organization of American States (OAS) imposed a trade embargo on Haiti.

The embargo quickly led to food and fuel shortages, a sharp increase in food prices, and a drop in economic output. The assembly industries were badly hit: 130 out of 180 manufacturing plants were forced to close down, since their supplies of raw materials were stopped and there was no power to run machinery. An estimated 32,000 jobs were lost.

In October 1993, when the Haitian military failed to implement an international agreement to allow the return of President Aristide, the

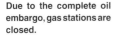

Due to the complete oil embargo, gas stations are closed.

United Nations Security Council responded by imposing a total oil embargo on Haiti. The embargo essentially paralyzed the economy by the end of 1993: imports and exports fell sharply, electricity supplies were down to a few hours per day, shops and other businesses were closed or operating on a part-time basis, and the prices of some basic goods had gone up 50%. The fuel shortage was reported to have caused the closure of even more assembly plants in the industrial park near Port-au-Prince.

By April 1994, there was still no end in sight to the embargo. Haitian ruling forces were alleged to have stockpiled more than 100,000 gallons of oil—some of it believed to have been diverted from emergency supplies—enabling the military to resist pressure from the international community for a considerable time.

While the deadlock continued, ordinary Haitians suffered widespread malnutrition and threatened famine, especially in rural areas. As an emergency measure, the United Nations resumed humanitarian fuel shipments to enable relief agencies and hospitals to survive.

The 1993 oil embargo severely affected the economy, causing a widening of the national deficit, a drop in international trade, and a plunge in the value of the gourde.

THE BARTER SYSTEM

Many Haitians do not use cash. Instead they get their daily necessities through the barter system. Usually farmers grow one or two types of vegetables, set aside what they need for themselves, and exchange the rest with other farmers for different kinds of vegetables or rice, or with shop owners for clothes and shoes. In order to buy the items that cannot be bartered, farmers sell some of their farm produce by the roadside for cash.

Conditions on Haitian roads— most of which are unpaved—go from bad to worse during heavy rain.

TRANSPORTATION

In Port-au-Prince, one distinctive form of transportation is the *publique* ("puh-BLIK"), a shared taxi that picks up several passengers along the way. Everyone pays the same fare, regardless of the distance traveled, and the nearest passenger is dropped off first. *Publiques* are easily recognizable by the red ribbon they display on their rearview mirror or radiator cap and the letter "P" on their license plate. There is also a network of urban buses, but service to the suburbs and shantytowns that have sprung up around the capital is not regular.

For rural travel, most people use *taptaps* ("TAP-taps"), Haiti's colorful public buses. However, peasants still walk long distances on foot, often without shoes. Small boats and ferries, though typically extremely slow and treacherously overloaded with people, animals, and cargo, are the most common method of transportation from one coastal village to another.

TRADE UNIONS

The labor union movement was legally recognized for the first time in 1948, but growth has been quite slow because of the relatively small number of industrial workers and professionals compared to farmers and rural laborers. There is only one labor federation, the National Union of Haiti, with a membership of over 3,000. About 10,000 other workers belong to 22 independent unions.

Minimum wages are fixed by law, but women generally make less than men for the same job. The constitution provides for fair wages, health protection, and social security. In practice, however, Haitian workers have very few rights.

HAITIAN INGENUITY

A brilliant testimony to the ingenuity and artistic talent of the Haitian people, *taptaps* are one of the most colorful means of public transportation in Latin America and the Caribbean. *Taptaps* are old Japanese-made trucks or vans that have been converted into public buses. Painted with images of mermaids, animals, flowers, or futuristic spaceships, they look more like circus or gypsy caravans. Decorations on the truck body may include stars, diamonds, and squiggles in red, green, and gold—the more flamboyant they are, the greater the driver's status. The simple wooden frame on the back is usually painted red and carved into graceful curves.

On each side of the truck, and sometimes on the back frame too, a Creole phrase, often religious, is displayed for all to read and ponder: "Thanks to the Invisible," "Father Joseph," "Divine Power," or "God Bless Nissan." The writing is illuminated by colored flashing lights. Often there is also a biblical scene painted on the hood of the truck.

Taptaps are usually overflowing with women carrying huge baskets of vegetables and fruits, men with poultry, children, and even an odd goat or dog.

HAITIANS

HAITI'S ORIGINAL INHABITANTS, the Arawaks, were peace-loving farmers and hunters who were driven off the island by the warlike Caribs before the arrival of the Spanish settlers. No indigenous people remain, however, and today's population of 6.75 million is almost entirely made up of the descendants of some 500,000 African slaves who were brought to Haiti to work on the plantations.

Whites and mulattoes—Haitians of mixed African and European descent—are minorities, together making up less than 10% of the population but holding most of the country's power and wealth.

Shop fronts bearing Arabic names reveal the presence of another minority: Syrians, fleeing persecution from the Turks, migrated to the Americas at the end of the 19th century and settled in Haiti. Most arrived penniless but soon became successful shopkeepers and merchants.

Opposite: **Haitians are a friendly and cheerful people despite the considerable hardships they continue to face.**

Left: **Among black rural Haitians, it is the woman who holds responsibility for the family's affairs.**

47

Most Haitians are poor, whether they live in the city or the countryside.

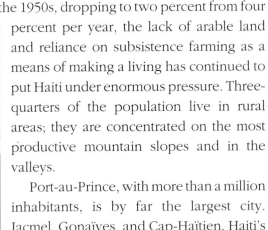

POPULATION PRESSURES

Haiti has more than 500 people per square mile, one of the highest population densities in the world. Despite the fact that the population growth rate has halved since the 1950s, dropping to two percent from four percent per year, the lack of arable land and reliance on subsistence farming as a means of making a living has continued to put Haiti under enormous pressure. Three-quarters of the population live in rural areas; they are concentrated on the most productive mountain slopes and in the valleys.

Port-au-Prince, with more than a million inhabitants, is by far the largest city. Jacmel, Gonaïves, and Cap-Haïtien, Haiti's other three main towns, have less than half a million people between them. Migration to the urban centers tends to be low, as urban unemployment is high and city life is just as harsh as in rural areas—most Haitians prefer to try and eke out a living on their tiny plot of land in the countryside. Because of the high level of land ownership, migration between rural areas is almost negligible. Most of the people who do move to the city, especially Port-au-Prince, are women who take jobs in the manufacturing or service sectors.

MULATTOES

Descendants of European colonists and African slaves, mulattoes now control the government, the army, and most of the professions—in other words, the destiny of the country. Mulattoes have less influence in business and commerce, as trading was traditionally seen as a mercantile occupation that was beneath the educated middle and upper classes. However, this attitude is changing as mulattoes realize how much there is to be gained financially from business enterprises.

To the mulatto, skin color is very important. Those with a lighter skin tone are considered by fellow Haitians to be more intelligent and generally superior. In the 18th century, Haitians developed elaborate tables of genetic descent, dividing mulattoes into over a hundred shades of black and white: these ranged from the *Sacatra* ("sah-kah-TRAH"), which is seven-eighths black, to the several varieties of *Sangmêlés* ("sahn-may-LAY"), which are only one-sixteenth black. Strictly speaking, the term mulatto applies to someone who is half black and half white.

Today, mulattoes are still very conscious of class divisions, and even within such a small group, there are differentiations based on skin color, wealth, and behavior. Mulattoes thus strive to be as French, as white, and as Westernized in their lifestyle as possible.

Despite a common heritage with blacks, mulattoes do not feel any sense of racial kinship with them; far from helping blacks improve their lot, mulattoes typically treat them with disdain and contempt.

This mulatto woman, her baby, and her mother-in-law demonstrate the varying skin tones among Haitians.

49

Haiti's population is predominantly young.

THE BLACK PEASANTRY

When they were slaves, Haiti's predominantly black population had no rights and were treated like animals. After independence, they were still poor, tied to a harsh land that yielded very little food for their families. The lot of today's black peasant has not changed much. Although free to move about, they are still slaves to the land and to their poverty.

Black Haitians' distrust and dislike of whites and mulattoes is deep-rooted. After having been oppressed for so long, first by the European colonizers, then by the Americans, and finally by the Haitian mulatto elite, it is not surprising that most black Haitians are wary of any moves that could be interpreted as attempts to subjugate them. The strong resistance to the landing of American police monitors in October 1993 is the most recent example of this.

Although Catholicism and the French language officially reigned supreme throughout most of Haiti's history, it is the voodoo religion and the Creole language—both unique Haitian adaptations of their African and European roots—that pervade the life of the black Haitian.

SLAVE ANCESTRY

The ancestors of most of today's Haitians were Africans, brought to the New World as part of the notorious Triangular Trade, which saw ships set sail from Europe, trade money and trinkets for slaves in Africa, unload the slaves in the Caribbean, and then return to Europe full of sugar and other commodities. Some Africans were seized by slave-hunters during night raids, while others were taken as prisoners of war during tribal wars and later sold to the European slave traders. Most slaves came from the Coromantee, Eboe, Mandingo, and Yoruba tribes. Chained to each other, they were thrown into the ship's hold, where the ceiling was so low they could not even sit up. At sailing time, members of the crew stood by with lighted torches and threatened to set fire to the ship if anyone attempted to escape. Once their homeland was no longer in sight, the slaves were allowed to come up on deck for a few minutes of exercise, always chained in pairs. Conditions were so atrocious that more than one in ten died during the trip, which took between six and twelve weeks. Some were struck down by disease, others committed suicide. A few days before arrival in the New World, the slaves were fed well to fatten them up, and their bodies were rubbed with oil to make them look healthy. Once off the ship, they were paraded through the streets of Port-au-Prince before being taken to the market for auction.

SEEKING REFUGE ABROAD

Throughout Haiti's tumultuous past, hundreds of thousands of Haitians have fled their homes seeking refuge in countries that offer greater political stability and a better standard of living.

The first wave of emigration out of Haiti came during the American occupation, when poor and dispossessed peasants were "invited" to work in Cuba and the Dominican Republic. The Americans at that time owned large sugarcane plantations in these two countries and were short of labor. Most migrants to the Dominican Republic have more or less assimilated into the local society.

In the second wave were professionals and educated Haitians fleeing the repressive Duvalier regime. Teachers, artists, politicians who opposed Papa Doc's policies, and administrators of international organizations were granted asylum in cities such as Paris, New York, and Montreal. They were later joined by skilled workers and technicians.

The emigration of skilled workers and trained professionals has only made Haiti's economic and social problems worse. Given Haiti's bleak prospects, however, it is not surprising that these emigrants left, and it is unlikely that they will soon return to their homeland.

The most recent wave of emigrants includes manual workers, taxi drivers, and laborers. Most of these are living abroad illegally, especially in the United States.

In all, it is estimated that more than one million Haitians are living outside their country. Every year 10,000 Haitians are admitted into the United States to join relatives already living there. A similar number are accepted into Canada. About 300,000 Haitians are living in New York City alone, while another 30,000 live in Miami.

Emigration to France is a more recent phenomenon. Often illegal immigrants manage to get into France from Haiti via one of France's overseas territories, such as Martinique, Guadeloupe, or French Guiana.

Over a million Haitians have emigrated to North America and Europe.

HAITIAN DRESS

Typical of the Caribbean, Haitian clothing is extremely colorful and made of light-weight cotton to suit the tropical climate. In the urban centers, men wear short-sleeved shirts and cotton trousers; women usually wear full skirts and simple wide-necked blouses in bright colors and patterns.

Clothing takes up a big chunk of poor families' income; women typically sew their family's clothes themselves from the cheapest available materials. When Alaska became part of the United States, an enterprising American businessman started exporting obsolete 48-star flags to Haiti at rock-bottom prices. Soon after, many Haitian families could be seen sporting the old American flag on their backs.

Rural Haitians have a set of clothes that they reserve for special occasions. Shoes are also kept preciously. Some going to Port-au-Prince walk barefoot and carry their shoes to the edge of town before putting them on. At home or in the fields, most of them are barefoot or wear homemade sandals fashioned out of whatever materials are at hand—even old automobile tires.

Most Haitian women wear light, loose clothing and wide-brimmed straw hats.

LIFESTYLE

THE HAITIAN LIFESTYLE is one of poverty, hard work, simplicity, community spirit, and—whenever possible—celebration.

The overwhelming majority of the Haitian population belongs to the urban and rural lower classes. Both live in humble, often one-room dwellings, believe in voodoo, have very little education, join together in common-law marriages, and speak Creole. At the other end of the social spectrum, upper-class Haitians live in grand houses, practice Catholicism, speak French, and are educated abroad.

The middle class is still a very small segment of Haitian society. Composed of both blacks and mulattoes, middle-class Haitians are less concerned about color and family background and tend to emphasize education and the use of French in order to progress professionally and improve their standard of living.

Opposite: **A Haitian woman transports her chickens to market.**

Left: **Middle-class families see education as a means of achieving a higher standard of living.**

SOCIAL DIVISIONS

UPPER CLASS The Haitian upper class makes up less than 5% of the population. It is composed mostly of mulattoes, but well-educated and wealthy blacks are also included. Upper-class Haitians are Roman Catholic, lead a Westernized lifestyle, and show an appreciation of all things French. They emphasize elegance and refinement in everything they do. Most socializing takes place after church on Sundays and in private clubs.

The elite lives in a closed, almost caste-like society. Membership in the group is almost always determined by birth. Elite people marry among themselves. The upper-class family is one where the parents are legally married and the mother stays at home to look after the children.

The elite lives and works in the cities. Its members own much of the urban land, which they rent out to the people working in factories and offices. The men favor the more gentlemanly professions of law, medicine, and architecture. Most women, although often well educated, do not work outside the home.

The family has remained the focal point of love and loyalty. Since the group is so small and intermarriage is the norm, most people are related to one another.

Wealthy Haitian men like to dress formally in a suit.

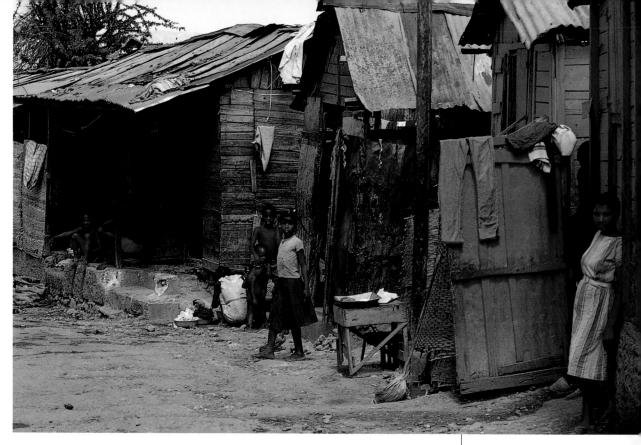

MIDDLE CLASS The middle class is a relatively new phenomenon in Haiti, brought about by wider educational opportunities and industrialization. Since the Duvalier period, the size and political clout of the middle class has continued to grow. Middle-class families see education as a means of achieving higher status. They speak French and typically work as civil servants, shopkeepers, technicians, and teachers.

URBAN LOWER CLASS The urban lower class makes up about half the urban population. Most members of this class came to the cities in search of work and now live in the slums that proliferate on the edge of town. Unemployment is high and many people work for themselves, scraping a living as lottery ticket sellers, artisans, or market women. Those who have a job are mostly employed in the service sector, as domestics, shoe shiners, or day laborers. The urban lower class work extremely hard to try and achieve a better standard of living. Their communities still display some aspects of rural living; people are always ready to help one another, and communal activities are common.

Shantytowns around Port-au-Prince are a maze of huts made of mud, scrap metal, and cardboard.

"The rich black is a mulatto; the poor mulatto is a black."

—*Haitian proverb*

A Haitian peasant considers himself lucky if he has a donkey, a few chickens, and a pig.

RURAL LOWER CLASS Peasants make up almost 90% of the Haitian population. They are at the bottom of the social ladder and most live in abject poverty. They grow their own food and live in huts made of a few sheets of corrugated iron nailed together; the huts have few, if any, modern amenities. Authority is held by the eldest male member of the family, although it is usually the woman who runs the family's day-to-day affairs.

A few peasants own larger land holdings and consequently have a better standard of living. They are called *gro neg* ("groh NEGG") or *gro zabitan* ("groh zah-bih-TAHN"), both expressions meaning a person of wealth and power. They are usually the leaders in their communities and become the local *chef de section* ("shef deh sec-SIOHN"), serving as a link between the local and the national governments.

Very few rural Haitians have access to running water, and clothes are washed in a nearby river or stream.

TONTONS MACOUTE

In 1958, President François Duvalier set up a private police force to consolidate his power and protect himself against the army, which he feared. First called the Milice Civile ("mih-liss sih-VIHL," or Civilian Militia), the force's name was changed to Volontaires de la Sécurité Nationale ("voh-lohn-tair duh lah say-cuh-rih-tay nah-sioh-NAHL," or National Security Volunteers), better known as *Tontons macoute*, or just *macoutes*.

Macoutes were characterized by their unswerving loyalty to the president and the use of extreme violence. Their tactics included torture, kidnapping, and murder, and their activities were above the law. At the height of their reign of terror, there were around 10,000 *macoutes* spread all over the country. A hardcore group of 2,000 was based in Port-au-Prince. Most were drawn from the urban

black lower class and were personally selected by Duvalier. Rural *macoutes* wore a uniform of faded blue denim and carried old rifles with cartridge belts, while urban *macoutes* dressed in shiny blue suits and tucked their pistols into belts or armpit holsters.

As only the trusted elite within the force was paid a salary, *macoutes* had the right to extort money from the population and to accept bribes. At the daily roadblocks they operated in and around Port-au-Prince, they exacted a toll from all motorists. A *macoute* also had the right to force his way into any house and demand to be fed.

After the fall of the Duvalier regime in 1986, *macoutes* were hunted down by a population enraged by decades of terror, and many were lynched in the streets. The force was officially disbanded, but plainclothes squads of *attachés* ("ah-tah-CHAY"), modeled on the *macoutes*, operate under the control of Haiti's chief of police. The United Nations Security Council has called for the disarming of *attachés*, who are believed to be responsible for the October 1993 blockade of international police monitors and for the murder of unknown numbers of Haitians.

Schoolgirls take pride in wearing their uniform. Although elementary education is compulsory, 80% of Haitian children drop out before the end of elementary school.

EDUCATION

Although public education is free, textbooks and other school materials are not, and as a result, many children, especially those in rural areas, cannot afford to go to school. Almost 90% of the population is illiterate, and this figure is not likely to go down much in the near future. The dropout rate for all levels is very high, especially in rural areas.

The best education is offered by private schools. Most private institutions are run by religious groups, such as the Roman Catholic Church and certain Protestant denominations. Some religious organizations offer a complete range of education from kindergarten through high school.

ELEMENTARY Kindergartens are operated by elementary schools and are the most attended of all schools. Children go to kindergarten for two years, generally at the age of three or four, and then move on to elementary school for another six years. Instruction is in Creole until the last few years, when children start learning French to prepare them for high school education.

HIGH SCHOOL Only about 10% of all children enrolled in an elementary school go on to a high school. There are very few high schools in the countryside—children may have to walk several miles to get to the nearest school—and classes are typically large. Rural children who graduate from elementary school often move to town to continue their education. Some vocational schools have boarding facilities, and the government gives out scholarships to defray the cost of lodging. High school education lasts seven years with a very demanding national examination at the end; many students drop out in the last two years. Instruction is in French and rote learning is the norm. About a quarter of the high school population attends vocational schools.

UNIVERSITY There is only one university in Haiti—the University of Haiti. Entrants must have a certificate of high school education, and some faculties hold entrance exams. The university does not offer postgraduate studies. Enrollment has declined in the past decade and the dropout rate is high. Children of well-to-do families usually go overseas for university studies, mainly in the United States, Canada, and France.

Vocational schools offer three-year courses that train students for technical jobs in industry.

HEALTH AND WELFARE

Haiti has more than six million people, yet there are only 600 qualified physicians.

Healthcare is a problem in Haiti as most homes do not have running water and people have to go to the river for personal and household washing. Regular contact with polluted rivers and streams puts Haitians at risk of developing chronic diseases carried by waterborne germs and parasitic worms. Malaria is also prevalent. Most Haitians suffer from nutritional deficiencies bordering on malnutrition. Life expectancy on average is only 54 years, and infant mortality is 11%. The death rate among children between the ages of one and four is even higher.

Medical facilities are poor and most are located in the urban areas. Most rural dwellers consult a voodoo priest when they need medical help, which only aggravates matters in some cases. There is one hospital bed for every 10,000 inhabitants. Supplementing the public health system, there are a number of clinics, mostly in villages and shantytowns, usually run by religious groups. Public hospitals and outpatient treatment are free, but patients must bring their own food and buy their own medical supplies.

MALNUTRITION

Most Haitians eat only one small meal a day; their calorie intake is the lowest in the Americas. This lack of food and inadequate nutrition has led to the widespread occurrence of chronic and often fatal diseases. Kwashiorkor, a disease caused by the lack of protein, is widespread among children. Poor rural Haitian children are at least six inches shorter and 50 pounds lighter than American children of the same age, and most grow up into weak adults who have very little resistance to disease.

SUBSISTENCE LIVING

About 75% of the Haitian population lives below the poverty level as defined by the World Bank. Most of them are peasants who try to scratch a living out of an uncooperative land. Their lifestyle has remained virtually unchanged throughout the history of the country. Because most peasants own their own land, they find it very difficult to break away from their traditional way of life, thus perpetuating their dependence on the land and their poverty.

Plots are typically too small to enable farmers to grow sufficient food for their families. Widespread soil erosion and a lack of irrigation have reduced the productivity of the soil, making it even harder for farmers to grow what they need.

As families grow larger and land plots get divided, some people are left landless and have to resort to sharecropping—working for a farmer in return for some crops. This is the lowest status occupation for a peasant.

HOUSING

Housing for most Haitians is extremely basic. Barely 2% of Haitians have running water, and less than 30% have ready access to drinking water. Poor urban Haitians who are employed usually rent one or two rooms as living accommodation for their whole family, while those who have no job or income are forced to live in squatter shacks that are roughly nailed together from whatever scrap materials can be picked up from the local garbage dumps. These squatter shacks have neither running water nor electricity. Hundreds of thousands of Haitians live in shantytowns, some of which are so overcrowded that huts are literally built one on top of another.

A Haitian farming shelter made out of straw. Most rural houses are made out of similarly humble materials.

Houses in rural areas are built of wattle covered with a layer of mud or plaster and are whitewashed. Floors are made of pounded earth, and the roof is usually covered with straw or sheet iron. Very basic kitchen facilities are located outside the house. Furnishings, in rural areas as well as in urban working-class areas, are sparse and simple. In large families, children sleep on mats on the floor.

Upper-class Haitians, on the other hand, live in ornate mansions with gingerbread wood embellishments and ironwork filigree, or in large new houses built of stone or concrete in the European style with all the modern amenities.

WOMEN

At the lower end of the social stratum, women play a vital economic role, shouldering much of the responsibility of providing food, income, clothing, and comfort for the family. Although men clear and prepare the fields for planting the family's food supply, women are responsible for growing the crops, transporting them, and selling them at the market. Women usually also have the responsibility of raising poultry and cattle, which they again take to market. Lower-class rural women thus control almost every aspect of their families' domestic affairs.

Market stalls are tended almost completely by women. These market women are popularly known as Madams Sarah, after a cheeping bird.

Upper-class women are typically well educated—often abroad—but they usually do not have to work for a living. This is gradually changing, however, as increasingly difficult economic conditions and the desire for economic independence have led more and more upper- and middle-class women to join the work force, usually as teachers, nurses, bilingual secretaries, and other professionals.

Although Haitian women were granted the right to vote in 1957, few women have succeeded in politics. Ertha Pascal-Trouillot, the first and only female Haitian head of state, headed the interim government for a short while after the fall of Jean-Claude Duvalier. Today, however, with the military in control, it is almost impossible for a woman to achieve political success.

RELIGION

ROMAN CATHOLICISM was the only official religion in Haiti for centuries after the Spanish first landed on the island. Nevertheless, black Haitians continued to keep alive the religious beliefs and practices of their African ancestors, and voodoo was finally recognized as an official religion in 1987. Roman Catholicism is generally only observed by upper- and middle-class Haitians.

Other religions have also made their presence felt in Haiti; American missionaries intent on converting Haitians away from voodoo—a religion they openly scorn and equate with the devil—have increased their activities at the grassroots level. Mormons (missionaries in the Church of Jesus Christ of Latter-day Saints), Baptists, Methodists, Jehovah's Witnesses, and Seventh Day Adventists all have missions in Haiti.

Opposite: **Voodoo, the "people's religion," is expressed through dance and song. Participants of these rituals dress in vivid costumes that sometimes include a headdress.**

Left: **Dressed in their finest clothes, two Haitian men make their way to a funeral on donkeys.**

ROMAN CATHOLICISM

Roman Catholicism did not gain as strong a foothold in Haiti as in other Latin American countries. As early as 1805, the Haitian constitution had separated church and state, and had declared marriage to be a civil rather than a religious contract. For 45 years after independence, no priest set foot in the country. Nevertheless, Catholicism was the only official religion in Haiti until 1987.

Catholicism today is observed mainly by the mulatto elite. To them, the Catholic religion is part and parcel of the French culture to which they aspire. The Church has become a symbol of their link with the outside world and a defense against the voodoo religion of the black masses. The

"Something must change in this country—poor people of all kinds must learn how to hope again."

—Pope John Paul II during his visit to Haiti in March 1983

Even priests in their immaculate white robes wear straw hats to shelter themselves from the harsh Haitian sun.

upper classes look upon voodoo as a kind of black magic practiced by ignorant people.

Church services are also something of a ritual for the upper echelons of Haitian society who see Sunday Mass as one of the main opportunities for socializing among themselves. Men dress in suits and women wear elegant dresses and hats to go to church every Sunday morning. After Mass, the men gather together to talk about business and politics, while the women exchange family news in the churchyard.

As Catholicism has traditionally been closely associated with the mulatto elite, black nationalists have always opposed the Church. François Duvalier had a running battle with the Roman Catholic clergy during much of his term in office. This culminated in him expelling from Haiti several provincial bishops and the bishop of Port-au-Prince, who was considered by Catholics to be the country's religious leader. Duvalier, in turn, was excommunicated by the Vatican.

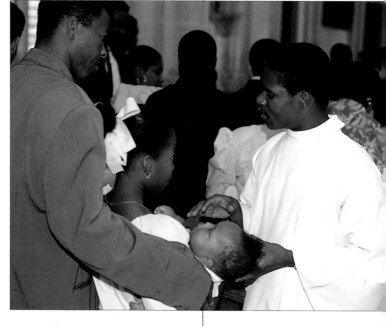

Middle-class Haitians baptize their child in the cathedral in Port-au-Prince.

Since then, the Catholic Church has done much to bridge the gap with the common people in Haiti. Priests now take an interest in the peasantry and have adopted a more pragmatic attitude to voodoo. The election of Jean-Bertrand Aristide, a Catholic priest, to the presidency increased the importance of the Church.

VOODOO

Voodoo is the national religion of the Haitian people and a vital force in politics and culture. Derived from African ancestor worship, voodoo has fused various African beliefs and rites with Catholicism to become a uniquely Haitian religion. Unlike other religions, it has no centralized church, no scriptures, and no theology. It is an informal religion of action, created by Haitians to suit their rural lifestyle. Voodoo is based on a mixture of superstitions and is celebrated through song and dance.

The concept of sin does not exist in voodoo. A person who acts in the wrong way does not offend the gods, but rather fellow human beings who suffer the consequences. Social and moral behavior is regulated by a set of taboos linked to ancestral values and traditions.

VOODOO COSMOLOGY The concept of God as a supreme being is not important in voodoo. Rather the voodoo cosmology is populated with *loas* ("LWAH"), or spirits that human beings can communicate with through possession or trance. The distinctions between divine and mortal beings are blurred; one can become the other through possession. The human body is animated by a *gro-bon-ange* ("groh-bohn-NAHNGE") and a *ti-*

"Haiti is 90% Catholic and 100% voodoo."

—Haitian folk expression

A VOODOO PRIESTESS IN NEW YORK

At the age of 12, Magritte Alexandre suddenly fainted when she received her First Communion. Her family believed that her fainting fit was an act of possession by a *loa*, a white spirit named Danbala. Some years later, Magritte was initiated into voodoo and left Haiti for the United States. Deeply religious, she is now a *manbo* ("mahn-BOH") serving the Haitian community in New York City, mainly as a faith healer.

bon-ange ("chih-bohn-NAHNGE"). These represent the soul and the cosmic consciousness. Upon death, the *gro-bon-ange* goes through several stages to become a *loa.*

The *loas* of African origin are called Rada, and those of Haitian origin Petro. The three most important *loas* are Legba, Erzulie, and Danbala. Legba is the *loa* between humans and their gods. He is invoked before any voodoo ceremony is held. Erzulie is a female *loa,* closely resembling the Virgin Mary of the Catholic Church. Danbala is also a female *loa,* in charge of rainfall. Her symbol is a serpent, which unlike the Christian symbol, is not evil.

VOODOO HIERARCHY The leaders of voodoo religion are priests and priestesses called *houngan* ("hoon-GAHN") and *manbo.* Both sexes are equal, although the more demanding ceremonies are usually carried out by male priests. Voodoo priests and priestesses have other jobs outside the priesthood and perform voodoo ceremonies as a service to the people. During voodoo ceremonies they are attended by a group of helpers called *hounsis* ("hoon-SEE").

A *manbo,* or voodoo priestess, telling fortunes.

A group of Haitian voo-doo worshipers pray to Nigerian gods.

VOODOO RITUAL Voodoo ceremonies are held to ask the blessing of a particular *loa*, to raise the spirit of the dead, or to place a curse on someone. The service usually takes place in a small enclosure with a thatched roof, often in the garden of the *houngan* or *manbo*. The temple is divided into two, with the inner chamber reserved for the priests and the initiated. The participants usually remain in the antechamber where most of the ceremony is conducted. Patterns called *vevers* ("veh-VAIR") are drawn on the floor in cornmeal to ward off evil spirits. The walls are hung with pictures of Catholic saints, flags, and stylized designs. A small altar holds sacred objects: ceremonial clothes, vases, and vessels containing baked earth, rattles, and bells.

The Catholic influence is strong in the opening ceremony with the voodoo priest blessing those present and everyone kneeling and making the sign of the cross. The *loa* is invoked by the priest to the sound of beating drums and rattles. Meanwhile the participants sing and dance in trance-like movements. The *loa* usually makes its wishes known through the *houngan* or the animal sacrificed. Possession by a *loa* is a desirable conclusion to the ceremony because it is interpreted to mean that the *loa* has spoken through the chosen person's mouth, revealing divine will.

THE GODS

Voodoo gods have close equivalents in African religions and in Catholicism.

Nigeria	Dahomey	Haiti	Catholicism
Eshu/Elegba	Legba	Legba = crossroads	St. Anthony St. Michael St. Peter
Obatala	Dahn-Wedo	Danbala Wedo = Batala = wisdom	St. Patrick Jesus Christ Lady of Mercy
Shango	Heviosso	Shango = Heviosso = storms, fire	St. Jerome St. Barbara
Ogun	Ogu	Ogou-Feray = war, iron	St. George St. Peter
Oshun	Ezili	Erzulie-Freda = love	Virgin Mary, Lady of Caridad del Cobre
Yemoja		La Sirène/Agwe = life-giving water	Our Lady of Peola Mary, Star of the Sea
Ibeji		Marassa = dualism/twins, ancestors	St. Cosme St. Damian
Oya		Gran Brigit = death/life	St. Catherine St. Teresa Our Lady of Candelaria

When talking about people, Haitians prefer to refer to them as "the man" or "the other person." Using the person's name in public has magical overtones.

FOLK MEDICAL BELIEFS

A zombie feels no pain and suffering and has no capacity for moral judgment, deliberation, and self-control.

When Haitians do not feel well, they usually do not go to a hospital or a clinic. Sickness and death are attributed to supernatural causes, so Haitians believe that only a voodoo priest can cure them. As a form of preventive medicine, people wear amulets given to them by their priest.

The Haitian people have perfected the science of using plants and herbs to cure sickness, and the use of herbal medicines is widespread. Chamomile is used to reduce swellings and tumors; hogwood bark to promote urination; soursop as a sedative; the wild plum leaf to reduce chills; and cedar bark to treat diarrhea.

Some medical beliefs are less benign and can be health-endangering. Voodoo priests sometimes advise that cow's milk is "too strong" for infants, that goat's milk is bad for infants, and that meat of all kinds is not good for the young. All these beliefs only serve to increase the problem of malnutrition among Haitian children.

ZOMBIES

A zombie is a body without a soul. Haitians are not afraid of zombies, but would rather not encounter them. Their greatest fear is to become one themselves. In the soulless zombie, the Haitian sees everything that is despicable: loss of the powers of perception and loss of self-control. For a Haitian, no fate is more terrible.

To prevent a person from being turned into a zombie, Haitians make sure that a dead body is truly lifeless before burying it. The corpse is stabbed in the heart with a knife; a plant with many seeds is placed in the coffin; the water used to bathe the corpse is carefully poured into a hole; and the hair and nails are clipped and buried alongside the corpse.

PROTESTANT MISSIONARIES

The most influential Protestant denomination in Haiti is the Episcopal Church, which has entrenched itself firmly among the lower classes since the mid-1800s. A black American priest from Connecticut, Reverend James T. Holly, established the first Episcopal Church in Haiti in 1861. Local artists were encouraged to paint biblical scenes inside the churches, and today there is a fine collection of biblical art in Protestant churches across the country.

The Baptist Church is one of the many Protestant denominations with missions in Haiti.

When François Duvalier wanted to establish a counterforce to the conservative and pro-upper-class Roman Catholic Church, he facilitated the work of American Pentecostal missionaries in Haiti.

Christian missionaries from the United States continue their campaign against voodoo and Haiti's indigenous culture even today. Lately there has been an enormous influx of Protestant denominations, mostly from the United States. With large finances at their disposal, they attract a lot of hungry and destitute people, putting them to work at their missions in return for food.

The Episcopal Church is very active in the field of education, running more than 50 rural elementary schools and two high schools in Port-au-Prince. It also has the distinction of operating the only school for handicapped children in the country, the St. Vincent's School for Handicapped Children.

LANGUAGE

HAITI HAS TWO national languages: French and *Kréol* ("kray-OHL"), or Creole. Virtually every Haitian understands and speaks Creole; French is spoken only by a small minority. Creole is the language of everyday life, while French is the language of refinement, a passport to social promotion. The use of language in Haiti highlights the polarities in society.

For more than a century after independence, French was the only official language of the country, even though an overwhelming proportion of the population could not understand it. It was only in 1969, during the presidency of François Duvalier, that Creole was granted legal status.

Above: **This sign reads "No entry" in Creole. It is particularly important for traffic signs to be in Creole, as the vast majority of Haitians cannot read French.**

Opposite: **Haitian street signs are in French.**

HAITIAN PROVERBS

Haitian Creole is a lively and colorful language. It expresses the very soul of the Haitian people, their wisdom and sense of humor. Creole conversation is sprinkled with proverbs that tell of fatalism and resignation, and of the cunning and carefulness needed when faced with the powerful in Haitian society:

> On an unlucky day, sour cream might break your skull and a sweet potato peel might cut your foot.

> Do not insult the crocodile's mother before crossing the river.

> The donkey does the work, while the horse gets the medal.

FRENCH

Even though French was the only official language of Haiti until 1987, less than 10% of the population speak it. At the elementary school level, the medium of instruction is Creole in the first few years, and children learn French almost as a foreign language. In high school, classes are conducted solely in French. As less than 20% of Haitian children complete elementary school, it is not surprising that their knowledge of French is so limited.

Given its exclusivity, French is considered by Haitians to be a sign of superiority; its use is restricted almost exclusively to the urban upper and middle classes. French is always used on formal public occasions and sometimes at formal private functions as well. Upper-class Haitians speak French whenever they meet—in church, at the club, and at other social

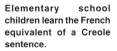

Elementary school children learn the French equivalent of a Creole sentence.

Every Haitian who speaks French can also speak Creole, yet only one in 10 Creole speakers know French.

GREETINGS

Haitians are a warm and hospitable people. A huge billboard proclaiming "Welcome to Haiti" in French greets visitors to the island, and it is typical for Haitians to smile and call out *"Bonjour, Blanc!"* ("bohn-djoor BLAHN"), or "Hi there, white!" whenever they bump into a Caucasian visitor on the street. Haitians are careful to show respect to each other, despite their characteristic lack of formality. When visiting friends, they say *"Honneur"* ("on-NERH") or "Honor" when they arrive; the host replies with *"Respect"* ("reh-SPAY"), or "Respect."

events. At home they are likely to speak both French and Creole, sometimes using words from both languages in the same sentence.

For the urban middle class, the use of French is seen as essential to moving up the social ladder. Middle-class Haitians always insist on speaking French, even in informal settings, to prove that they are worthy of belonging to the upper class, and they make sure their children do not speak Creole—something they see as a "bad habit" of the lower classes.

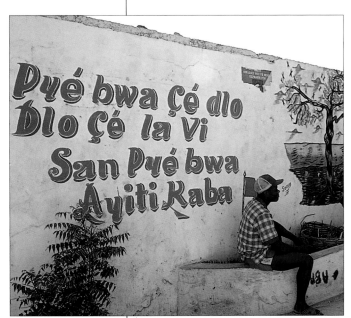

Creole, the "people's language," is an important educational tool. This mural warns Haitians about the environmental consequences of cutting down too many trees.

CREOLE

Haitian Creole was originally a lingua franca, or pidgin, used as a means of communication among the Haitian slaves, who spoke a number of different African languages, and between slaves and their French-speaking masters. Now a full-fledged language with its own grammar and spelling system and the sole language of most Haitians, Creole is finally recognized as one of Haiti's official languages.

STANDARDIZATION OF CREOLE

At first Creole was only a spoken language. Its vocabulary was made up of French and African words pronounced in a distinctive Haitian way, but there was no standard spelling system. Although some writers wrote in Creole in the early 1920s, they spelled words arbitrarily, according to their own conventions.

It was not until the early 1940s that an attempt was made at devising a standardized spelling. Two Americans, Ormond McConnell and Frank Laubach, established a phonetic alphabet in which each sound was represented by a single symbol. This system was later modified by French linguists Charles-Fernand Pressoir and L. Faubles using certain conventions of the French alphabet. Present-day Creole grammatical structures and spelling developed from these early works.

CHARACTERISTICS OF CREOLE   Haitian Creole is a very dynamic language, reflecting foreign influences and characterized by the invention of new words and structures. Although most words are of French origin, African and Spanish words have also left their mark, and Creole grammar and syntax are influenced by African grammatical structures. Haitian Creole is also a linguistically economic language: thoughts and actions are expressed using a minimum of words, determinants and prepositions are used sparingly, and words are simplified. When certain long words are shortened, they become the same as other short words, so intonation is very important in helping to distinguish between words.

CREOLES AROUND THE WORLD

Creole languages spring up when groups of people who speak different languages make contact with each other and need to develop a quick way of communicating without learning each other's native language. As Europeans explored other continents, set up trading relations with other peoples, and transported slaves from Africa to the New World, a number of Creole languages based on European languages developed around the world.

From English came Gullah, spoken off the coast of South Carolina, Sranantongo, spoken in Suriname, and Pidgin English, which still flourishes in Melanesia (New Hebrides, the Solomon Islands, and New Guinea), Hawaii, and Papua New Guinea. From French there are the Creoles of Haiti, Louisiana, and the Lesser Antilles, and from Pidgin Spanish and Portuguese there is the Papiamento of Curaçao. Easier to learn than the native languages of so many different countries, Creole languages are often indispensable as a means of communication, an educational tool, and in politics.

Spoken by 90% of Haitians, Creole has always been seen by nationalists as the "real" language of Haiti. It thus became an ideological symbol, a vehicle of protest against the ruling class of mulattoes. Not surprisingly, François Duvalier, who rose to the presidency on a platform of black power, was a strong supporter of Creole.

Haiti has several daily and weekly newspapers.

NEWSPAPERS

The first newspaper in Haiti was published in 1764. *Affiches Américaines* ("ah-fish ah-may-rih-KEN") reported on commercial, cultural, and agricultural events. Today, there are two daily and four weekly newspapers published in French and one monthly publication in English. Two newspapers are nearly a century old: *Le Nouvelliste* ("luh noo-vehl-LIST"), founded in 1898, and *Le Matin* ("luh mah-TEHN"), established in 1907. Haitian newspapers have mass appeal, focusing on local gossip, cultural events, and sports news, and are generally quite small, ranging from four to eight pages.

Because of government censorship, domestic news is presented from the government's point of view and foreign news is limited, with only AFP (Agence France Presse) providing an international service. Little space is given to crime news, and political news is confined to official releases.

CENSORSHIP

The history of the press in Haiti is characterized by a rigorous system of censorship and repression. Even though freedom of the press has been guaranteed constitutionally since 1972, editorial immunity has never become a reality. Newspapers are not allowed to publish anything that could be construed as criticism of the government. Throughout Haitian history, journalists have been persecuted, imprisoned, shot, and exiled for falling afoul of the ruling party.

RADIO AND TELEVISION

Since the national daily newspapers are limited to the Port-au-Prince area and very few Haitians can read, radio is more important than print in disseminating news throughout the country. There are several radio stations, most of them privately owned and operating regionally. Broadcasts are in French and Creole. However, the vast majority of the population still does not own a radio and thus has no access to public information.

There is one television station that broadcasts on two channels. Operated commercially, its programs can be received only in the Port-au-Prince area. The station operates only in the evening and broadcasts in French. In 1989, a mere 25,000 television sets were estimated to be in use in Haiti.

Widespread poverty and illiteracy mean that the teledyòl, *("tay-lay-DIOHL"), or grapevine, is the most common—though not the most reliable—way of spreading news in Haiti.*

ILLITERACY

Haiti's literacy level is the lowest in the Western Hemisphere: only 10% of the population knows how to read and write. As a means of comparison, the literacy rate in the neighboring Dominican Republic is 60%, and this figure is considered low by Caribbean standards.

The abysmal literacy rate is largely the result of Haiti's poor educational system. Before independence, there were no schools in Haiti—the colonialists simply sent their children to France to be educated. Haiti's first post-independence ruler, Jean-Jacques Dessalines, was illiterate himself and failed to recognize the importance of education. After independence, the state continued to neglect education, providing only a minimal elementary and high school system and doing little to improve the poverty that forces so many Haitian children to abandon school at an early age.

ARTS

AN INNATELY ARTISTIC people, Haitians have successfully married the culture of their African ancestors with French influence to produce a unique Haitian style. Whether painting pictures, buses, churches, houses, public buildings, or simply lampposts, Haitians adorn their world with unrestrained and brilliant color. Even the Casernes Dessalines—the notorious military barracks where so many Haitians have been tortured— is drenched in pure yellow, creating a magnificent contrast with the intense blue of the sky. From the inter-city *taptaps*, or public buses that display a collage of flamboyant decorations, homespun proverbs, and religious quotations, to the voodoo dancing that is performed both as a religious celebration and to welcome tourists to the elegant old villas of Port-au-Prince, Haiti displays a deep and varied artistic spirit.

Opposite: **Boisterous bands, called rara bands, pound drums, whirl batons, and blow into long, bellowing bamboo tubes.**

Left: **Many Haitian bus paintings are a work of art.**

Drummers abound during a carnival.

MUSIC AND DANCE

The Haitian soul comes alive in dancing. In Haiti, dancing to the beat of the drum is a means of communication as well as a celebration of life.

Young children dance, old people dance, everyone dances in Haiti. They dance to celebrate a festival, to express their gratitude for a bountiful harvest, or to forget their poverty.

Haitian music and dancing have changed very little since the days of slavery on the sugar plantations. Most dances were born of voodoo, and a voodoo ceremony always concludes with a dance. Today there is ritual dancing as well as dancing *pou plaisi* ("poo play-ZEE"), or for leisure. One Haitian dance that has achieved international recognition is the meringue. An eye-catching dance with sinuous and languorous movements, it is enjoyed by the elite and the urban lower classes alike. The songs that accompany the meringue are often full of innuendo concerning love or politics.

Haitian music, like other Caribbean varieties, is based on four beats. However, local musicians bring in variations that alter the rhythm. In the meringue, for example, a weak beat always follows the strong salvo of drums.

MUSICAL INSTRUMENTS

Haitian music is defined by the sound of the drum. Drums are used in both religious and secular performances. The standard sacred drum used in voodoo ceremonies is the *rada* ("rah-DAH"). Always in a set of three, the *rada* is made up of the *mama* ("mah-MAH"), the largest drum, which is struck with a wooden hammer; the *seconde* ("seh-GOHND"), which is struck with a *baguette* ("bah-GET," a bow-shaped piece of wood strung with a cord); and the *boula* ("boo-LAH") or *kata* ("kah-TAH"), the smallest of the three, which is hit with two sticks.

Rada drums are usually painted in the colors of the spirits to which they are dedicated and are easily recognizable by the wooden pegs or knobs inserted below the rim of the head to tighten the skin. Carnival drums come in three types: a conical one about three feet high tightened by crisscrossing ropes; a small cylindrical hand drum hung from a cord around the neck of the player; and a double-headed drum, beaten with sticks or bare hands.

A distinctive instrument is the *marimboula* ("mah-rim-boo-LAH"). It is a box-like instrument with an opening in the face across which are fastened steel thongs of varied length and corresponding tone differences. The player sits straddled across the box while alternately or concurrently plucking the steel bands and beating the face of the box with the palm of the hand.

Other instruments used in Haitian music are rattles, guitars, trumpets, and scrapers. Carnival boys blow the *granboe* ("grahn-BOH"), trumpets made from three- or four-foot long joints of bamboo.

The Spanish tambourine is as popular in Haiti as in the other Caribbean islands. The thumb of the right hand is covered with powdered resin and then drawn in a rapid spiral circling the face of the tambourine. The result is a humming roar that can be heard from far away.

"A Haitian could accurately be described as one who sings and suffers, who toils and laughs, who dances and resigns himself to his fate. With joy in his heart or tears in his eyes he sings."

—*Jean Price-Mars*,
Thus Spoke the Uncle

LITERATURE

In the 19th century many educated and wealthy Haitians devoted themselves to the study of fine arts in the classical French tradition. At the beginning of the 20th century, however, the literary focus shifted to native Haitian folklore and literary values.

Haitian writers often used poems and essays to express their nationalistic fervor and deep anguish at foreign domination. Jean Price-Mars was an innovator in Haitian literature who supported the concept of *négritude* ("nay-grih-TUHD")—pride in being black and in the African heritage. His novel *Ainsi Parla l'Oncle* ("ehn-sih pahr-lah LOHNCL," *Thus Spoke the Uncle*), which was published in 1930, was the first Haitian novel to explore the life of the country's black peasants.

Louis Diaquoi, a leading journalist and poet, believed that Haitian writers should draw inspiration from their African heritage. He fostered the literary group Les Griots, whose basic source material comes from voodoo and of which François Duvalier was a member.

BOOKMAN EKSPERYANS

One of Haiti's most popular bands, Bookman Eksperyans ("ayks-pair-IAHNS") is openly critical of the military government and has had several songs banned from Haitian radio and television. Band members are very vocal in their support for a revolution in Haiti and have expressed their desire to see a *lakou* ("lah-KOO") system in place. *Lakou* is the symbol of deep family roots and traditions, a tie to the land and place, and a sense of commitment and community.

In 1992, when the group performed a concert in honor of the group leader's father, 500 soldiers showed up with their guns prominently displayed. As Bookman Eksperyans was about to perform the banned song *Kalfou Danjere* ("kahl-foo dahn-DJAIR," *Dangerous Crossroads*, censored for its incendiary lyrics), the soldiers started pulling out their guns.

Leon Laleau, a versatile writer who used both prose and poetry, portrayed the deep despair of his people in a literary piece, *Le Choc* ("luh SHOK," *The Shock*). His *Musique Nègre* ("muh-zik NEGR," *Negro Music*) is an excellent collection of verse expressing the heart and soul of the Haitian masses. The most famous Haitian writer, however, was Jacques Roumain, poet, novelist, and ethnologist. His novel, *Gouverneurs de la Rosée* ("goo-vair-NUHR duh lah roh-ZAY," *Master of the Dew*), is a powerful and realistic portrayal of life in a peasant community. It has been translated into 17 languages.

Women have always been active on Haiti's literary scene. Virginie Sampeur, Ida Faubert, and Lucie Archin-Lay were noted poets and essayists. The novelist Marie Chauvet, who died in 1973, was a major voice in Haitian literature.

Haitian literature was born of anger directed against the white masters of the colonial past.

CITY OF POETS

Jérémie, a small town on the north coast of Haiti's southern peninsula, was a flourishing mulatto town before François Duvalier ordered the massacre of all mulattoes there. With its community of amateur writers and artists, Jérémie was known in its heyday as the City of Poets.

One of the most distinguished of these poets was Edmond La Forest, who is renowned for the sonnets he composed in honor of prominent 19th century writers such as Baudelaire, Edgar Allen Poe, and Arthur Rimbaud. La Forest committed suicide in 1915, on the anniversary of the assassination of Haitian general and emperor Jean-Jacques Dessalines. A later great poet from Jérémie was Emile Roumer, who came from a Franco-Haitian family of nine brothers. Well read in the works of classical French writers, as was La Forest, Roumer was also influenced by surrealism. He distinguished his poetry from that of Francophiles such as La Forest by celebrating the beauty of black Haitians and mocking the mannerisms of his own mulatto society.

PAINTING

There are more than 800 recognized painters in Haiti, most of them self-taught, working full-time, and painting in a variety of styles. A unique style of painting is the Primitive movement, a naive style making use of bright colors and depicting the daily life of the Haitian population. This movement started in 1944, when DeWitt Peters, an artist and teacher from the United States, encouraged the renaissance of Haitian art by opening the Centre d'Art in Port-au-Prince. Within a few years, Haitian Primitive paintings received international recognition, and several outstanding Haitian paintings now form part of the permanent collection of New York City's Museum of Modern Art.

A modern painter at work.

A painting by Valcin II entitled "The Birth of Democracy" portrays different elements of Haitian life.

Philomé Obin, considered the founding father of the Primitive movement, was the first renowned Primitive painter; his masterpiece is entitled the *Funeral of Charlemagne Peralte*. But the greatest Primitive painter was probably Hector Hyppolite, a poor voodoo priest who painted doors, windows, and buildings to earn a living. Every now and then, he used left-over house paint and brushes made from chicken feathers to paint pictures. His work was discovered in 1945 by DeWitt Peters. Hyppolite was brought to Port-au-Prince where he remained a prolific painter until his death in 1948.

Mural painting is also very popular. The movement was started in 1949 by Selden Rodman, an American poet and art critic. Huge murals can be found on everything from church cathedrals and hotel walls to airports and exhibition sites.

The Episcopal Church gave a boost to Haitian painting when it commissioned the Centre d'Art to decorate its churches. The most acclaimed mural is Wilson Bigaud's *Miracle at Cana*, in which the New Testament feast is placed in a Haitian setting and embellished with such details as a policeman chasing a thief. This mural adorns the Episcopal Cathedral of the Holy Trinity in Port-au-Prince.

ARCHITECTURE

Haitian architecture is a contrast of African heritage and French colonial style. When it comes to color, however, the style is pure Caribbean; Haitians reveal their imagination, love of fun, and lack of inhibitions as they cover all available surfaces with the sun-drenched hues of their tropical surroundings. Walls, doors, shutters, roofs, trim—even lampposts and garbage cans— are painted with diamonds, squares, stripes, and solid panels in vividly contrasting colors.

Climate plays an important role in Haitian architecture. As in many Caribbean islands, houses in Haiti are sited in such a way that they can benefit as much as possible from the cooling trade winds blowing from east to west.

Certain architectural elements also help cope with the extremely hot weather— peaked roofs increase the protection from sun and rain, cutout trim filters out the bright sun while still allowing air to pass through, and unglazed attic windows provide ventilated storage space for the family's harvest.

As in other French- and Spanish-influenced islands, balconies and front porches directly overlooking the street are common features, enabling Haitians to socialize easily with their neighbors. On narrow city streets, houses usually include a store or warehouse on the street level, while the family residence is located on the floor above.

In the countryside, people live in *cailles* ("KAEE"), which are simple, often one-room houses with roofs made of hay or corrugated iron.

All dwellings, whether rural or urban, are decorated with brightly painted doors, shutters, and woodwork.

In the wealthy and cooler suburban residential neighborhoods of the cities of Jacmel and Port-au-Prince, houses are set in large gardens and are characterized by elegant gingerbread fretwork, delicate and ornate wooden or iron balconies, extravagant bell towers, and windows outlined in brick archways. Entire interior walls are sometimes covered with elaborately carved redwood panels.

Vibrant, contrasting colors and strong graphic designs are typical in Haitian architecture. Each house expresses the personality of its owner, and no two houses are the same.

Cap-Haïtien, Haiti's former capital, still has fountains, forts, and fine stone bridges built in the colonial style. One of the most beautiful examples is the neoclassic parish church of Cap-Haïtien built in the 18th century. The stately white National Palace and other public buildings all point to Haiti's colonial past.

THE EIGHTH WONDER OF THE WORLD

Built as the crowning glory of King Henri Christophe's reign, the Citadelle Laferrière is the largest fortress ever built in the Western Hemisphere. Standing at the peak of a 3,000-foot mountain, the Citadelle can only be reached by mule.

Eccentric King Christophe, who ruled the north of Haiti from 1807 to 1820, was a great builder of castles and palaces. He built the Sans Souci Palace at the base of the mountain as a private retreat, but he embarked on the Citadelle with a loftier purpose in mind—it was intended to be a fortress against a French invasion.

Sitting on top of a mountain and shaped in an irregular square, the Citadelle Laferrière tapers to a prow. The walls, 80–130 feet high and 20–30 feet thick, surround a central parade ground, and 360 huge cannons guard all approaches. The fortress was designed to contain a garrison of 10,000 soldiers.

Work on the Citadelle started in 1804 and continued sporadically for the next 15 years. It is alleged that 200,000 people were put to work on the fortress and over 20,000 of them died from exhaustion during construction.

But King Christophe's dream of seeing the building completed never came true: in 1821, the people revolted against him and he committed suicide. His wife and a loyal courtier carried his body to the Citadelle and dropped it in a vat of quicklime in the courtyard—at least fulfilling his wish of being buried in his fortress.

The Citadelle Laferrière was never completed and has never been used. Still, it is Haiti's most revered national symbol, a monument to the lives sacrificed in the struggle for freedom.

Designated by the United Nations as one of the world's cultural treasures, the building is considered by some to be the eighth wonder of the world. However, neglect and the effect of the tropical climate have taken their toll: the stone-and-mortar structure is in dire need of repair.

Some nights King Christophe would work alone on the walls of the Citadel Laferrière, reliving his younger days as a stone mason.

SCULPTURE

Haitian sculpture blends African artistic heritage with the spontaneity and creativity of an uprooted people. Odilon Duperier, a former carpenter's assistant, excels in carved masks and figures. Jasmin Joseph is best known for his lively and imaginative terracotta sculptures and for the choir screen he created for the Holy Trinity Cathedral. Georges Liataud and Murat Brière, the foremost Primitive sculptors, specialize in sheet iron sculpture. Using scrap iron from old gas cans, they produce amazing sculptures blending reality and fantasy. One sculptor who makes use of a rather unusual medium is Roger François. This highly talented artist carves strikingly human faces out of dried roots.

This wooden carving portrays Haitians' love of playing music and singing.

LEISURE

SOCIAL ACTIVITIES for the elite in Port-au-Prince revolve around private clubs that offer dancing, banquets, golf, tennis, and swimming. For the vast majority of Haitians, however, much simpler and less expensive pleasures are enjoyed in the house of the voodoo priest that serves as a kind of community center. The most common leisure activities for the peasant are the voodoo ceremony, which always involves singing and dancing, and the cockfight, the national "sport."

Haiti's widespread illiteracy has led to a strong oral culture, and storytelling is another extremely popular form of entertainment. Every region in Haiti has its *maître conte* ("met COHNT"), literally a "master of stories," who wanders from village to village recounting stories and folktales that have been passed down from generation to generation.

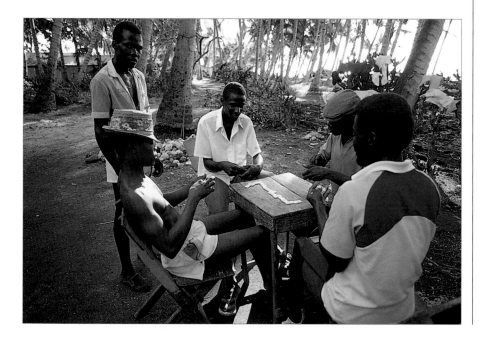

Opposite: **Haitian men love to gamble.**

Left: **Playing dominoes is a popular way of passing an afternoon or evening.**

Haitian boys demonstrate their skill in passing at a neighborhood soccer match.

SPORTS

The most popular sport played in Haiti is soccer, although the game has never aroused the same type of passionate following in Haiti as it has in some other Latin American and Caribbean countries.

In the countryside, children who cannot afford to buy a proper soccer ball are content to kick a substitute made of rags around an empty patch of ground. Competitive soccer is generally restricted to Port-au-Prince where regular matches take place at the national Sylvio Cator stadium.

In general, conventional sports play only a limited part in recreational life, as they all require some form of equipment or location the average Haitian cannot afford. Tennis, for example, is only played by the urban upper and middle classes.

GAMBLING

The popularity of gambling and games of chance is the result of the Haitian's belief that so much depends on the fancy of the gods. Winners of bets are seen as the lucky ones chosen by the gods. Thus gambling is not only an attempt to make some money, but also an attempt to know the wishes of the gods.

Gambling is a predominantly male activity. Even the peasant occasionally makes a tiny wager on some game of chance. Large sums of money are won and lost in the casino in Port-au-Prince, open only to the well-to-do.

The rest of the population makes wagers on cockfights, bullfights, card games, or dominoes.

The most popular form of gambling is the lottery. Imported from the Spanish Antilles, the *loterie-borlette* ("lot-tree bohr-LET") has superseded all other forms of gambling in Haiti. Tickets for the weekly draw are sold in all major centers.

Dreams and minor incidents of daily life are interpreted in terms of winning numbers. A car accident attracts huge crowds who buy lottery tickets based on a combination of the numbers on the license plates. During voodoo ceremonies, Haitians implore the gods to reveal winning lottery numbers.

Gambling tables and lottery booths are found at every street corner in Port-au-Prince; many Haitians are likely to spend their last gourde trying to hit the jackpot.

COCKFIGHTING

The closest thing to a national sport in Haiti is cockfighting. From March to December, cockfights take place every Sunday morning all over the country. The fighting pit is a kind of arena with terraced wooden benches all around, called a *gaguère* ("gah-GAIR").

Only roosters are used in cockfights, and only men are cock-trainers. Fed all year with raw meat and hot peppers soaked in rum, the animals are aggressive and tough. The cocks' skin is rubbed with ginger to harden it, and the neck, feet, and rump are massaged with mahogany bark. The sharp spurs the animals wear on their claws can inflict fatal wounds on the opposing cock. To increase the chances of winning, they are given war-like names by their owners: *Tambou mèt* ("tahn-boo MEHT," Drums of the Master), *Foc sé malhè* ("fok say mah-LAIR," There's Going to be a Disaster), or *Consul pangnol* ("kohn-suhl pahn-NYOHL," Spanish Consul).

A cockfight usually ends with the death of the losing cock. Attended by people of all classes, the bouts evoke from spectators the frenzied enthusiasm that is lavished on soccer in many Latin American countries.

Dancing under the *tonnelle*. The *tonnelle* is symbolic of the communal lifestyle of rural populations. Almost a town hall, wedding feasts and all happy occasions take place there.

BAMBOCHE

The *bamboche* ("bahn-BOSH") is a social get-together with no sacred significance. In town, *bamboches* are usually held at a rum shop, bar, or brothel. Men pay to enter the establishment or buy rum in return for a dance with the women (usually prostitutes). Most of the customers are young or middle-aged men. They come to the *bamboche* not for the dancing, but to meet people or pick up prostitutes.

The country *bamboche* takes place under a *tonnelle* ("toh-NELL"), a simple structure of poles supporting a banana-thatched roof. The whole village gathers together to have a good time. The dancing is free, except for special occasions when money is collected for a feast. Money is also collected to buy rum. Participants usually buy refreshments and snacks from street vendors.

As the *bamboche* is a social occasion for people to meet, group dances are preferred. The dance is led by a dance master, usually the best dancer in the neighborhood. As older people are typically more skilled, they tend to be the leaders and the younger ones follow. The usual dances are congo pastoral, meringue, rumba, and bolero.

COMBITE

At a *combite*, everyone chips in. Music and singing make the work go faster, and when it is done, there is food and dancing.

As Haitian peasants cannot afford to pay people to work for them, they get together in a *combite* to help each other. On the appointed day, friends, relatives, and neighbors turn up at a person's house or field and help build a house or bring in the harvest. The helpers are not paid, but are offered rum and food after the job is done. Everyone sings as they work under the direction of an appointed leader. When a great number of workers are involved, they divide themselves into two teams and compete to see which team finishes first. Work ends in mid-afternoon, and the feast may conclude with a dance.

In another form of *combite*, a group of workers go from place to place to help farmers. The *combite* then becomes a roving dance, stopping at the houses or farms of neighbors to assist in planting, reaping, or house-building. To the rhythm of singing and drum beating, the *combite* assumes the *chario-pie* ("shah-rio-PIEH") movement, a constant halt and run. At the end of the day, everyone gathers under the *tonnelle* for a *bamboche*.

The *combite* is an essential part of rural life. It has both an economic and a social function, helping to knit the rural community into a self-helping society.

OSSELETS

Osselets ("oss-LAY") is a kind of ball-and-jacks game, but played with goat's knuckles. Five *osselets* are used, each having four sides: *dos* ("DOH"), *creuse* ("KREUHSE"), I, and S. All five pieces are thrown in the air and left to land on the ground. The player then picks up one *osselet* and throws it in the air and picks up another one before catching the first one in the palm. Before picking up an *osselet*, the player has to turn it on its *dos* side first.

The aim is for each player to pick up an extra *osselet* each time until all five are in the palm. The player who achieves this first wins the game. If an *osselet* falls on the ground before the other one is picked up, then it is the next player's turn to play. Every time a player drops an *osselet*, he or she has to start from the beginning again.

FESTIVALS

ENJOYING FESTIVALS comes naturally to Haitians. Their sunny disposition leads them to always seek out a reason for rejoicing despite their considerable poverty and suffering.

A look at the calendar on page 110 gives an idea of the numerous festivals celebrated in Haiti. Christmas, Mardi Gras, the Day of the Dead—every religious and secular event provides an opportunity for the Haitian people to bring out their musical instruments and start singing and dancing. A drum or a guitar, a bottle of rum, and perhaps a colorful homemade costume are all that are required and are within almost everyone's means.

Haitians celebrate festivals with wild abandon, forgetting for a while that they are poor and have next to nothing.

Opposite: **A Haitian in full carnival splendor.**

Left: **Pilgrims immerse themselves in mud during the Plaine du Nord festival.**

CHRISTMAS

Christmas is a big event in Haiti. Everyone goes to Midnight Mass on Christmas Eve and then goes home for a celebration dinner and Christmas gifts. Even the most destitute family makes an effort to prepare a special dinner.

As in most of the Christian world, Haitian children believe that if they have been good, Santa Claus, or *Bonhomme Noël* ("boh-nohm NOEL"), will visit and bring them presents. If they have been bad, however, *Père Fouettard* ("pair fooay-TAR") will leave a whip that their parents will use to beat them.

CHRISTMAS SIGHTS

Months before Christmas, children begin working on their *fanal* ("fah-NAHL"). Cardboard strips are glued together in the shape of a house or church. A design is drawn in pencil on the cardboard walls and the design is then carefully punched out with a nail. Colored paper is pasted on the inside of the walls; when a lighted candle or small kerosene lamp is placed inside the *fanal*, the pattern stands out like stained glass. On Christmas Eve, boys and girls carry their *fanal* in a procession around the streets of the town or village. It is a wonderful sight and many people come out on their doorstep to watch the procession. When they get home, the children place the *fanal* in the window so that passers-by can catch its glow.

Children also make nativity scenes at school. Cardboard figures of Joseph, Mary, Jesus, and the Wise Men are placed in the creche. In some country towns, large nativity scenes are built in the town square and may feature public figures, such as the mayor or the tax collector!

Christmas trees are not common; they are popular only among the rich urban upper class. The custom was left behind by the Americans who occupied Haiti before World War II. A more common sight is the decorated *tonnelle* in rural areas. Haitians hang gourds and strips of colored paper on the *tonnelle* to give it a festive atmosphere.

NEW YEAR'S DAY AND INDEPENDENCE DAY

New Year's Day is especially significant to the Haitians. Not only does it signify the beginning of a new year, but it is also the beginning of freedom in the country—January 1 is also Haiti's Independence Day. In recognition of the importance of the occasion, January 2 is also a public holiday.

Military parades are a common sight on Independence Day.

On New Year's Day, it is customary for entire Haitian families to gather for a special dinner of ham, liqueur, and cake. Housewives put out the best tablecloth and dinnerware. Everyone in the family puts on a new set of clothes and children receive gifts from their godparents.

The formal and solemn part of the holiday takes place in the morning. In every town square, wreaths and flowers are placed in front of the National Palace, at the foot of the Statue of the Maroon (a statue of a slave), a symbol of freedom for Haiti's black people. In Port-au-Prince, marches and military parades are organized in celebration of the country's independence from colonial rule.

On January 2, a tall pole is erected in the center of town and money and cakes are placed on top of the pole. Many young men try to climb the pole to get to the money and cakes, but the pole is greased and only the best athletes succeed in reaching the top.

MARDI GRAS

Merrymakers at the Mardi Gras, the highlight of Carnival, which is celebrated with four days of singing and dancing.

Carnival begins every year on January 6 and culminates in a four-day party that ends on Mardi Gras (Shrove Tuesday). Preparations begin as early as October, with adults and children making their own masks.

Every Sunday between January 6 and Lent, there are processions in the streets with carnival bands playing drums and trumpets, and singing. The bands dance their way down the street and people from all around join them, dancing and singing. Starting on the Sunday before Lent, the carnival starts to get more and more elaborate. There are parades with flamboyantly decorated floats, and wealthy families organize grand fancy dress balls. Some towns elect a King and Queen of the Carnival.

During Carnival, young boys run around in masks and costumes. Blowing whistles, they stop passers-by and offer them a look inside their *lamayote* ("lah-mah-YOT") in return for a few cents. A *lamayote* is a box containing a pet animal or "monster," usually a lizard, a mouse, or a bug.

Traditionally, Haitians burn their costumes on the last day of Carnival; in reality, all but the wealthy now save up their costumes for the following year.

SPRING FESTIVAL

The Spring Festival runs from May 1 to 4. Less elaborate than the Mardi Gras Carnival, it is usually celebrated with feasting and dancing. Each town features a parade, and even the mayor joins in the march.

Labor Day, or Agriculture Day, is part of the Spring Festival celebrations. It was first decreed a holiday in the 19th century by President Alexandre Pétion, who hoped to stimulate an interest in agriculture. In those days, the best laborer in each parish received a prize, while a child from the best-cultivated farm in the district was awarded free education by the state. Today there are no competitions, but the day is still observed as a holiday.

When people see the rara band leader, they shout, "Rara!" On Palm Sunday children follow the bands with palm leaves.

THE RARA

Rara bands appear during Lent, between Carnival and Easter. Wearing red shirts and carrying a red flag, they dance their way down the streets in the mountains and villages. Sometimes they carry a dead chicken on a stick or lanterns made of tins filled with kerosene.

Rara bands dance and sing accompanied by the beat of drums. For small gifts of money, they will dance for onlookers. The leaders are accomplished dancers dressed like jesters with brightly colored handkerchiefs and sequined capes. When two groups meet, their leaders sometimes challenge each other to competitive dances.

Near Jérémie, rara festivities include exhibitions by wrestlers, who are sometimes accompanied by their own musicians. During Holy Week, the rara carry an effigy of Judas from place to place. On Good Friday, the effigy is hidden and the community makes merry as it hurries about in search of the hiding place so the villainous effigy can be destroyed. The rara do not dance on Easter Sunday.

CALENDAR OF FESTIVALS AND HOLIDAYS

January 1	New Year's Day and Independence Day
January 2	Heroes of Independence Day
Variable	Mardi Gras
Variable	Shrove Tuesday
Variable	Good Friday
April 14	Day of the Americas
May 1	Labor Day
May 18	Flag Day
May 22	National Sovereignty
July 16	Saut d'Eau
October 17	Death of Dessalines
October 24	United Nations' Day
November 1	Toussaint L'Ouverture's Day
November 2	Day of the Dead
November 18	Armed Forces' Day
December 5	Discovery Day
December 25	Christmas

WASHING AWAY BAD LUCK

On July 16, the little town of Ville-Bonheur (Happiness Town) swarms with 50,000-strong crowds that have come from all over Haiti to celebrate the *saut d'eau* ("soh DOH," waterfall). The Virgin Mary is reported to have appeared at the top of a palm tree near the waterfall in the 19th century. Today tens of thousands of pilgrims come to pray to the Virgin and at the same time tell their sorrows to the voodoo gods. In long lines, they make their way to the rock where La Tombe River falls in a cascade. Standing under the gushing water, they hope to wash away their bad luck. One after another, silently, they come down from the waterfall with white powdered faces and tears streaming down their cheeks.

Nearby, the presence of gaming tables and the sound of beating drums give almost an air of carnival to the gathering. But this notion is quickly dispelled by the chorus of supplications coming from the parish church.

Haitians gather under the waterfall to wash away their bad luck at the annual Saut d'Eau festival.

THE DAY OF THE DEAD

Wakes and funerals are always occasions of social importance where the departed is entertained by feasting and drinking, storytelling, and the playing of cards and other games. But on November 2, the entire day is given over to celebrating and honoring the dead.

All Souls' Day, or the Day of the Dead, is one of the four biggest holidays in Haiti. People everywhere visit cemeteries with tributes of flowers and say prayers for their dead ancestors. At home, it is customary to *manger aux morts* ("mahn-djay oh MORH"), or offer food to the family's dead ancestors. Some people place the food on the ground, while others put it on the table where the dead person used to sit. A candle is lit and prayers are said. Only after the food has been offered to the dead does the rest of the family sit down to dinner.

On the Day of the Dead, shrines are set up to honor those who have died.

HARVEST DAYS

Harvest festivals best exemplify the influence of voodoo on daily life in Haiti. For two days in November, Haitian peasants celebrate *manger-yam* ("mahn-djay YAM"), literally "eat yam" day, a voodoo ritual that points to the importance of yam in the diet of the rural population.

One of the recreational high points of the year, *manger-yam* is celebrated with feasting, drinking, singing, and dancing. A voodoo priest performs a ceremony marked by incantations to the dead and to the voodoo spirits.

In the villages, families eat their dinner first before offering the leftover food to their dead ancestors.

QUACKS AND CHEATS

Crête à Pierrot is a fort located near the town of Petite-Rivière in the Artibonite Valley. On September 30 each year, people from all over the valley gather in front of the little church to celebrate the feast of the town's patron saint. Ignoring the ceremony inside the church, the pilgrims rattle off a list of wishes and supplications, sharing their sorrows and misery with fellow pilgrims.

After the church service, everybody proceeds to the fort. This is where the real pilgrimage starts for most people. A number of quacks and cheats are waiting for them there, ready to exploit the ignorance and misery of the poor peasants. For five gourdes, pilgrims can have a "leaf bath." The bath, according to the quacks giving it, washes away bad luck. For a few more gourdes, the patient can even take home some of the "holy" water in a little bottle for the family. In front of the fort's ammunition room, another cheat claims to reveal the spirit of the fort to whomever pays one gourde. As the spirit is a very potent one, the pilgrim should go in backward and communicate with it facing the door! Every year there are more quacks and cheats.

FOOD

AS IN SO many other aspects of Haitian life, the difference between rich and poor manifests itself in the quantity and quality of the food consumed by the different social classes. The urban elite eats sophisticated Creole meals, while the poor peasants often eat only one meager meal a day.

At its best, Haitian food is cooked with fresh ingredients and local herbs and spices, and has many special dishes that are on a par with the best cuisines in the world. The African, French, and Spanish influences on Creole cooking give Haitian cuisine an elegance and a variety that many believe is unmatched anywhere in the Caribbean.

Above: **Tiny carts all over Haiti sell drinks made from pouring different flavored syrups over shaved ice.**

Opposite: **A typical Haitian grocery store.**

AFRICAN SWINE FEVER

Many farmers rear pigs because these animals do not require much investment—pigs eat anything that is given to them, including household refuse. The pig is a valuable commodity to the Haitian peasant, and many Haitian dishes use pork as a principal ingredient.

In the late 1980s, when African swine fever hit the pig population, the Haitian authorities slaughtered all the peasants' hardy black Creole pigs. Less hardy white pigs were imported from the United States as replacements, but Haitians were either unable to afford the new pigs or saw many of them die from disease. Many farmers consequently suffered a drop in their standard of living.

THE HAITIAN DIET

The Haitian diet is high in starch. The staple foods are rice (grown locally in the Artibonite Valley since 1941), corn, millet, and yam. The Haitian national dish and mainstay of Haitian cooking is *pois ac duriz colles*

A food stall serving rice and beans, the national dish of Haiti.

("PWAH ack duh-rih COLL"), rice and beans. Most poor people eat *petit mil* ("peh-tih MILL"), or sorghum, which is pounded with a 20-pound pestle and cooked in an old, well-seasoned black iron bowl; every bit is scraped out for the family meal.

Green vegetables and tropical fruits grow well in Haiti, and a wide variety is available seasonally. However, vegetables do not make their way to the peasant dinner table very often as farmers usually need to sell their produce for money or trade it for goods rather than eat it themselves. For vegetables, peasants eat the wild greens that they gather in open fields. Citrus fruits, avocados, breadfruit, and mangoes grow in abundance and are eaten extensively when in season. Mangoes are of particular importance in the Haitian diet as they are rich in vitamin A.

Meat is almost nonexistent in the diet of ordinary Haitians because of its high cost. Farmers often rear their own chickens, but again they tend to sell the eggs and meat rather than eat them. The most common meats consumed are goat and pork. Fish and shellfish abound in the seas surrounding Haiti and in the rivers, but they are not popular outside Port-au-Prince.

ONE MEAL A DAY

Facilities are primitive in a typical Haitian bakery.

Peasants start the day at dawn with a breakfast of strong locally grown coffee, sometimes accompanied by a disk of sour bread baked from bitter manioc flour. (Bread made from imported wheat flour is almost non-existent outside urban centers.) A light lunch is eaten in the fields at midday. The principal meal of the day is eaten at home in the late afternoon with the whole family. It is usually the national dish of rice and beans, or a stew with a small piece of meat if the family's financial circumstances are favorable.

However, in the summer season, when the crops have not yet reached maturity, many rural people subsist on no more than one starchy meal a day, such as porridge made from corn, rice, or sorghum. To satisfy their hunger pangs, some people chew on sugarcane stalks or green mangoes.

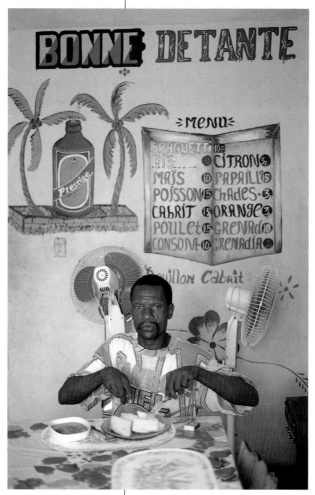

A man enjoys his food in a humble but brightly decorated restaurant.

CREOLE CUISINE

Much like the food of New Orleans, Haitian Creole cooking features distinctive recipes and subtle flavors imparted by the use of local herbs and spices.

Among the Creole specialties prepared in hotels, expensive restaurants, and upper-class homes are spiced shrimp, pheasant with orange sauce, green-turtle steak, wild duck, and salad made with hearts of palm.

Rice *djon-djon* ("jon-JON"), one of Haiti's rice-and-bean dishes, is found nowhere else in the Caribbean as it calls for an ingredient that is unique to Haiti—Haitian black mushrooms. The inedible stems of these small mushrooms are used to color the rice black; they are then removed and the mushroom caps are added along with lima beans.

Another traditional Haitian dish is *calalou* ("kah-lah-LOO"), a mixture of salted pork, crabmeat, pepper, onion, spinach, okra, and chili pepper. The ingredients are simmered for one hour or more and the dish is served with rice.

Other dishes are *tassot* ("tah-SOH"), a preparation of grilled meat, and *pain patate* ("paihn pah-TAT"), a pudding made of grated potato, figs, banana, and sugar.

Numerous sauces are used to spice up Haitian meals. The most renowned of these is *ti-malice* ("tih-mah-LISS"), an extremely spicy tomato and onion concoction.

Typical beverages include a mild variety of coffee that is grown locally and is mainly consumed by upper- and middle-class Haitians, soft drinks made of brightly colored syrups and shaved ice, and alcoholic drinks, such as whisky, brandy, and the locally distilled Barbencourt rum.

Some Haitian dishes are commonly found in New Orleans, thanks to the Haitian slaves who were brought in to work on the Louisiana plantations.

SAUCE TI-MALICE

This sauce is usually served with pork chops, but it also makes a delicious dip for French fries.

10 large ripe tomatoes, peeled and quartered
3 white onions, quartered
4 red hot peppers (Scotch bonnet or jalapeño), seeded
3 tablespoons brown sugar
1 tablespoon salt
2 cups malt vinegar

Purée the tomatoes, onions, and peppers in a food processor. Transfer to a large saucepan and add the brown sugar, salt, and vinegar. Stir well to combine.

Cook the sauce over moderate heat, stirring occasionally, until it begins to boil. Lower the heat and simmer the sauce for 20 minutes, continuing to stir occasionally.

Bottle the sauce in hot sterilized jars.

Rum factories convert sugarcane into a particularly potent type of rum.

SUGAR

Sugar is consumed in enormous quantities, helping to make up for the lack of calorie content in the typical Haitian diet, but not for the inadequacy of protein and vitamins.

Rapadou ("rah-pah-DOO") is a syrup produced in the refining process of sugar. It is used to sweeten drinks, tea, and coffee. *Rapadou* is also the base for *clairin*, the raw and concentrated rum that is the most popular alcoholic beverage among rural Haitians.

A large amount of sugar is also consumed by chewing stalks of sugarcane. Both adults and children pluck the stalks direct from the field or buy them at the market, tear off the leaves, and chew on the stalks with the bark still on, extracting the sweet juice. It is not only nutritious, but also refreshing in the hot Haitian climate.

True to their French origins, upper- and middle-class Haitians love sweets and pastries, and always keep them in stock. No dinner is complete without a sweet dessert such as rich mousse or ice cream.

THE MARKETPLACE

Markets are the center of economic and social activity in many towns and villages. In the Port-au-Prince area, market vendors make their way to one of the 23 markets as early as 5:00 a.m. Many women walk several miles carrying huge baskets on their heads to sell the produce they have grown and buy the food and manufactured goods they need.

The Iron Market, which is packed with thousands of Haitians every day, is the heart and soul of Port-au-Prince. In the countryside, markets are just a wide open space where women gather to trade their wares. Peasant women display their vegetables and fruits on tables and trestles in neat rows. Salted codfish and manioc flour are piled into towering mounds, and meat is sold in the open since there are no refrigerated containers.

In addition to food, a wide variety of other goods are offered for sale: fabrics, baskets, locally made cigarettes, contraband whisky, straw hats, cooking utensils and lamps made from old tin cans, spices, and rum. The marketplace is noisy and bustling with activity, with customers haggling over prices and sellers praising their wares.

Haitian women at a Jacmel market.

Prepared foods, such as bread, fried bananas, and grilled meats are also sold. The most popular market-stall dish is a porridge made with ground corn, sugar, and milk. It is cooked in a big tin can over a wood fire. Served in a tin cup and eaten on the spot with a teaspoon, this porridge is consumed at any time of the day.

121

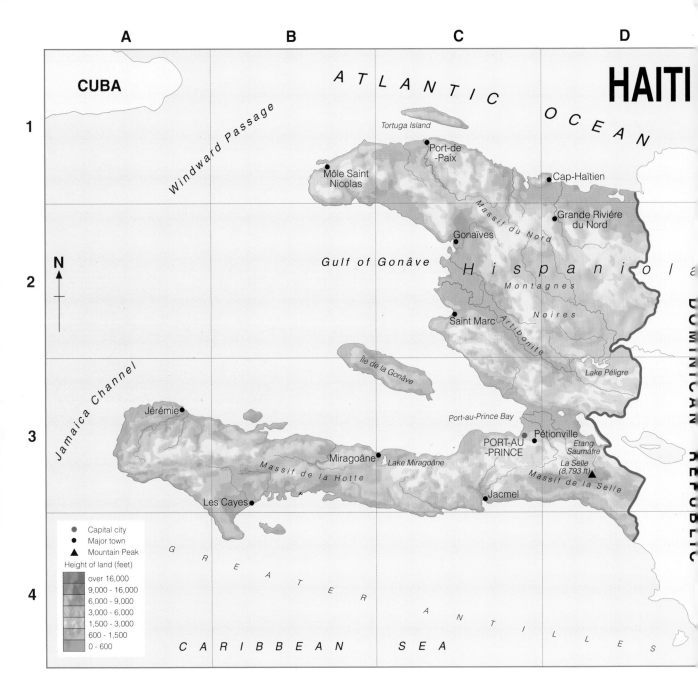

HAITI

CUBA

ATLANTIC OCEAN

Windward Passage

Tortuga Island

Port-de-Paix

Môle Saint Nicolas

Cap-Haïtien

Grande Riviére du Nord

Massif du Nord

Gonaïves

Gulf of Gonâve

Hispaniola

Montagnes Noires

Saint Marc

Artibonite

Île de la Gonâve

Lake Péligre

DOMINICAN REPUBLIC

N

Jamaica Channel

Jérémie

Port-au-Prince Bay

PORT-AU-PRINCE

Pétionville

Etang Saumâtre

Miragoâne

Lake Miragoâne

Massif de la Hotte

La Selle (8,793 ft)

Massif de la Selle

Les Cayes

Jacmel

G R E A T E R

A N T I L L E S

C A R I B B E A N   S E A

- ● Capital city
- ● Major town
- ▲ Mountain Peak

Height of land (feet)

	over 16,000
	9,000 - 16,000
	6,000 - 9,000
	3,000 - 6,000
	1,500 - 3,000
	600 - 1,500
	0 - 600

A   B   C   D

1

2

3

4

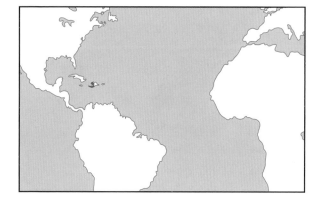

QUICK NOTES

OFFICIAL NAME
Republic of Haiti (*Répiblik Dayti*)

LAND AREA
10,714 square miles

POPULATION
6.75 million

CAPITAL
Port-au-Prince

MAJOR CITIES
Jacmel, Gonaïves, Cap-Haïtien

LONGEST RIVER
Artibonite

HIGHEST POINT
La Selle (8,793 feet)

OFFICIAL LANGUAGES
French, Creole

OFFICIAL RELIGIONS
Roman Catholicism, Voodoo

CURRENCY
Gourde, divided into 100 kobs
(5 gourdes = $1)

MAIN EXPORTS
Coffee, sugar, bauxite

MAIN IMPORTS
Foodstuff, machinery, fuel

INDEPENDENCE DAY
January 1

LEADERS IN POLITICS
Toussaint L'Ouverture, hero of
    independence
Jean-Jacques Dessalines, first ruler of
    independent Haiti
Henri Christophe, first king of Haiti
François Duvalier (Papa Doc), repressive
    president-for-life
Jean Bertrand Aristide, Roman Catholic
    priest, president-in-exile in New York

LEADERS IN THE ARTS
Jean Price-Mars (writer)
Leon Laleau (writer and poet)
Jacques Roumain (poet, novelist, and
    ethnologist)
Hector Hyppolite (painter)
Philomé Obin (founder of the Primitive
    movement in Haitian painting)
Odilon Duperier (sculptor)

GLOSSARY

affranchis ("ah-frahn-SHEE") Freed former slaves who were granted French citizenship.

bamboche ("bahn-BOSH") Social get-together with dancing and drinking.

combite ("cohn-BIT") A group of friends getting together to help people build a house or gather the harvest.

houngan ("hoon-GAHN") Male priest in voodoo.

lakou ("lah-KOO") A sense of commitment to the land and to traditions.

loas ("LWAH") In voodoo, spirits with which human beings can communicate and which exert an influence on human life.

manbo ("mahn-BOH") Female priestess in voodoo, proficient in faith healing.

rara Bands that sing and dance during Lent.

taptaps ("TAP-taps") Trucks converted into buses with colorful decorations; most common form of transportation in rural areas.

Tontons macoutes ("tohn-tohn mah-COOT") Private army set up by the Duvalier regime; known for its brutality.

voodoo "The people's religion," combining ancestor worship, African animist beliefs, and Roman Catholic rituals.

zombie A body without a soul, that will do the bidding of its master.

BIBLIOGRAPHY

Herbert Gold: *Best Nightmare on Earth: A Life in Haiti*, Prentice Hall Press, New York, 1991.

Richard A. Haggerty, editor: *Dominican Republic and Haiti* (2nd edition), Federal Research Division, Library of Congress, 1991.

Ute Stebich: *A Haitian Celebration: Art and Culture*, Milwaukee Art Museum, Milwaukee, Wisconsin, 1992.

Amy Wilentz: *The Rainy Season: Haiti Since Duvalier*, Simon & Schuster, New York, 1989.

INDEX

INDEX

INDEX